Aquinas on the Four Last Things

Other books by Kevin Vost
from Sophia Institute Press:

Memorize the Faith!

Fit for Eternal Life!

The One-Minute Aquinas

Unearthing Your Ten Talents

12 Life Lessons from St. Thomas Aquinas

The Seven Gifts of the Holy Spirit

The Catholic Guide to Loneliness

How to Think Like Aquinas

The Seven Deadly Sins

Hounds of the Lord

Kevin Vost, Psy.D.

Aquinas on the Four Last Things

Everything You Need to Know
about Death, Judgment,
Heaven, and Hell

SOPHIA INSTITUTE PRESS
Manchester, New Hampshire

Sophia Institute Press
Box 5284, Manchester, NH 03108
1-800-888-9344
www.SophiaInstitute.com

Sophia Institute Press® is a registered trademark of Sophia Institute.

Library of Congress Cataloging-in-Publication Data

Names: Vost, Kevin, author.

Title: Aquinas on the four last things : everything you need to know about death, judgment, heaven, and hell / Kevin Vost, Psy.D.

Description: Manchester, NH : Sophia Institute Press, [2020] Includes bibliographical references. Summary: "Summarizes and provides reflections on Thomas Aquinas's writings on the four last things: death, judgment, heaven, and hell"— Provided by publisher.

Identifiers: LCCN 2020042913 (print) LCCN 2020042914 (ebook) ISBN 9781644132999 (paperback) ISBN 9781644133002 (ebook)

Subjects: LCSH: Thomas, Aquinas, Saint, 1225?-1274. Eschatology.

Classification: LCC B765.T54 V64 2020 (print) LCC B765.T54 (ebook) DDC 236—dc23

LC record available at https://lccn.loc.gov/2020042913

LC ebook record available at https://lccn.loc.gov/2020042914

3rd printing

To
Henry and Marjorie Vost
and to
Pete and June Collins

"Man is debtor chiefly to his parents
and his country, after God."
—St. Thomas Aquinas,
Summa Theologica, II-II, 101, 1

Contents

Part 4
To Hell for Those Who Choose It

Acknowledgments

Many thanks to Charlie McKinney, John Barger, Nora Malone, Sheila Perry, Anna Maria Mendell, Molly Wierman, and all at Sophia Institute Press for giving me yet another chance to share the timeless wisdom of St. Thomas Aquinas with as few egregious errors and tiresome typos as possible. Any remaining infelicities may be traced back to my own keyboard.

Special thanks, too, to my friend Shane Kapler, who read an early version of the book and, as always, provided some very helpful feedback.

Last, but not least, I'd like to acknowledge the ongoing encouragement I receive from a precious and precocious young new family member. He began reading my books at age seven, and he always asks about them. A few days ago, one of the presents for his ninth birthday was a pack of black-light markers that write messages that are invisible until you shine an ultraviolet light on them. His first secret message to me read as follows: "How's your new book coming along?" Well, as you'll soon see when I hand you your copy, it's here, Sergiuz Cabal!

Aquinas on the Four Last Things

Introduction

The Most Important Things of All

*The treatise on the resurrection offers
a threefold consideration, namely the things
that precede, those that accompany, and
those that follow the resurrection.*

—*ST*, Supplement, 69, Prologue

*In all you do, remember the end of your life,
and then you will never sin.*

—Sirach 7:36

Last Things First

We tend to think of an end as something that comes last, and this
is certainly correct in the case of the Four Last Things—death,
judgment, heaven, and hell. They certainly do come last: at the
end of our lives and the end of the world. Indeed, *there is absolutely
nothing of greater importance to each and every one of us than how
and where we will spend eternity*, enrapt in the unspeakable bliss
of the Beatific Vision of God in heaven, or suffering unspeakable
torments in the presence of Satan, within the depths of hell. As
we see in our opening quotation, Yeshua ben Sirach, inspired

by the Holy Spirit, tells us that if we would always hold the Last Things foremost in our minds, we would never sin, out of our fear of hell and our loving desire to please God and reside with Him forever.

The Church's great teacher and "Angelic Doctor," St. Thomas Aquinas, often reminds us that proper actions are determined by their ends, that is, their ultimate goals or final endpoints. In this sense, an end is an organizing and motivating principle. St. Thomas and Sirach would certainly agree that reflection on the Four *Last* Things should make us increasingly mindful of the death, judgment, heaven, or hell that await us all at the end, and should provide for us a new *beginning*: a beginning of good choices, choices that abhor and reject sin while helping us grow in virtue and closeness to God during our brief time on earth.

If we are to *remember* and *reflect* on the Four Last Things and allow them to guide *how we live*, we must begin by seeking to *understand* them better. Thankfully, through His presence on earth, divine revelation, and the Church He founded for us, God has provided us with all kinds of aids to help us understand the final things that await us.

Among the greatest sons of the Church that God established is our aforementioned guide, St. Thomas Aquinas himself, who was blessed with an unparalleled capacity to understand important and lasting things. Thomas lived on earth from an unknown date in 1224 or 1225 until March 7, 1274. He now resides with Christ, reveling in the beatific bliss he sought to help us all attain through his writings while he was what he called a *viator*, or "wayfarer," here on earth (as are all of us in this life). Indeed, he seeks to help us even now from heaven through his prayers for us. It is St. Thomas's understanding of the Four Last Things that will form the backbone of this book (not to mention most of its flesh—and its heart and soul!).

The Four Last Things of the Summa Theologica

The most famous, most important, and, well, just plain most *enormous* of St. Thomas's books is the *Summa Theologica* (or *Summa Theologiae*, a title many modern scholars prefer), which clocks in at over three thousand pages, with 1.5 million words. This theological masterpiece, this "summary of theology," was designed to enlighten us with the best that human reason, drawing on its knowledge of the world and divine revelation, can tell us about God and creation, human nature and its fulfillment, and how Christ and His Church can lead us back to our Creator, so that we may experience the most glorious Last Thing of heaven.

Though he is called the "Angelic Doctor" in part because of his heavenly intellect, neither did Thomas write the *Summa* from scratch nor did he base it entirely on the fancies of his own mind. Rather, he borrowed from, compiled, analyzed, synthesized, and made wonderful sense of the greatest insights of the philosophers, theologians, saints, Church Fathers, and Doctors of the Church who came before him. Many of these great thinkers will be cited in the pages ahead to show how Thomas profited from their wisdom on the Four Last Things, and how we can too.[1] Indeed,

---

[1] To avoid a possible plethora of overwhelming detail in the text or footnotes, when quoting the Fathers and Doctors of the Church, I will usually not provide the exact reference in terms of which books and pages are quoted. I will always specify in which questions and articles of the *Summa Theologica* (*ST*) they appear. Passages from the *ST* can be tracked down easily by anyone

this is why Thomas wrote his massive *Summa* and began it with an explanation of theology as a "sacred science" through which the theologians of the Church employ their God-given reason, in cooperation with the intellectual gifts of the Holy Spirit (including counsel, knowledge, understanding, and wisdom), to guide us deeper into the meanings of Holy Scripture and the articles of faith, so that we may better understand and serve God.

In the centuries following Thomas's death, some Protestant theologians have argued against the need for the Catholic Church to explain the Faith. They have espoused instead the "perspicuity of Scripture"—the belief that the words of Scripture are so clear that any honest layman who is open to the guidance of the Holy Spirit can sufficiently grasp its meaning. How odd, then, that the Holy Spirit has subsequently led the members and leaders of thousands of non-Catholic Christian denominations into contradictory conclusions on matters of faith as vital as what we must do to be saved and whether, once saved, we can lose our salvation—not to mention diametrically opposed views on issues including infant Baptism; the nature and validity of the sacraments, including Christ's Real Presence in the Eucharist; and all four of the Last Things!

In the pages that follow, we will see the errors inherent in the notion that all the important lessons of Scripture are clear to all who read them. With the help of dozens of Church Fathers and Doctors, Thomas will show how easily a superficial reading of particular biblical passages leads to misinterpretations, and just how nuanced the meanings of some passages can be.

---

who either owns a physical copy of the *ST* or uses a free online version such as the one located at https://www.newadvent.org/summa/.

Indeed, Thomas notes in the first question of the *Summa* that Holy Scripture has *multiple levels* of non-contradictory meanings. Within the same sentence, Scripture can describe a fact and reveal a mystery. God can signify meanings not only in words, as men do, but also in things and events themselves. Thomas says that our interpretation of Scripture should start with its *historical* or *literal* sense. Based on the literal level is the *spiritual* sense, whereby one thing signifies yet another. Within the spiritual sense, elements of the Old Law that signify or point to elements of the New Law constitute the *allegorical* sense. The *moral* sense concerns what we ought to do and how we are to live. Finally, things that relate to our eternal glory (indeed, our primary focus in these pages) constitute the *anagogical* sense. Thank God for the Catholic Church, her Fathers, and her teachers, especially St. Thomas Aquinas, for helping us master as much of the truth of the Four Last Things as we can while on earth!

Unfortunately, St. Thomas left the earth and took his place in heaven before his greatest work was completed. His last written words are found in the *Summa*'s third and final part, which, in the edition I use most often,[2] concludes on page 2,561, a

[2]   Thomas Aquinas, *Summa Theologica*, 5 vols (Westminster, MD: Christian Classics, 1981). When I desire to examine closely Thomas's writing in the original Latin, as I will several times in the pages ahead, I consult the following excellent edition: St. Thomas Aquinas, *Summa Theologiae: Supplementum, 69–99*, trans. Fr. Laurence Shapcote, O.P., Latin-English Opera Omnia (Green Bay, WI: Aquinas Institute, 2017). For a more in-depth examination of some of Thomas's key terms, I consulted the following book: Roy J. Deferrari, *A Latin-English Dictionary of St. Thomas Aquinas: Based on the Summa Theologica and Selected Passages of His Other Works* (Boston: St. Paul Editions, 1986). Finally, here is a link for readers who care to review Thomas's

good 450 pages before the end of the book. Thomas had not yet specifically addressed the Four Last Things, yet in the last two hundred pages or so of the *Summa*, we find thirty-four questions, comprised of 164 articles, called the "Treatise on the Resurrection." How can this be?

Thankfully, Thomas's friends and disciples recognized the profundity and importance of this great unfinished symphony of a book: a book that would someday replace the highly esteemed *Sentences* of Peter Lombard (ca. 1096–1160) as the Church's foremost book of theology; a book that two centuries after its completion would sit beside the Scriptures on an altar during the Council of Trent. After Thomas's death, his devout, scholarly followers drew from his extensive writings, primarily his *Commentary on the Sentences of Peter Lombard*, to finish his "Treatise on the Sacraments" and to create the "Treatise on the Resurrection," wherein we find Thomas's writings on the Four Last Things.

St. Thomas begins his "Treatise on the Resurrection" by explaining that while his previous treatise in the *Summa* showed how the sacraments save us from the *death of sin*, this last treatise will show how the resurrection delivers us from the *death of punishment*. He will address the things that occur *before*, *during*, and *after* the resurrection. I assure you, the questions he asks and answers make for some very interesting reading. Here are some examples:

• Do our souls go straight to heaven or hell when we die?
• Are souls ever allowed to leave heaven or hell?
• Will children who die without Baptism suffer eternal punishment?

"Treatise on the Resurrection" (*ST*, Supplement, 69–99) in English online: https://www.newadvent.org/summa/5.htm.

- Where is purgatory in the Bible?
- Why should we pray *for* the dead and *to* the saints?
- Can we predict the time of the final judgment?
- Will sinners be "left behind" on earth?
- How old will our bodies appear at the resurrection?
- What four special gifts will perfect our glorified bodies in heaven?
- Will our glorified bodies glow?
- How could God, in His justice, punish us *eternally* for the sins we committed in our brief time on earth?
- Will the damned and the demons be released from hell one day?
- What kinds of rewards await us in heaven?
- Will we ever see God, the great "I AM," as He Is, in the essence of His Godhead?

This book will address all of these questions and more (a total of 164, to be exact), along with Thomas's answers. We will follow closely the format and content of that remarkable Thomistic treatise found in questions 69–99 of the Supplement to the *Summa*, as well as the three questions of its appendices. Our first chapter will present the material of question 69, which discusses the destination of our souls after death. From there, each chapter of this book, except for the final chapter of each of the four parts, will provide a rapid-fire summary, in simple, accessible language, of each successive question in Thomas's "Treatise on the Resurrection" within the *Summa* (except for the questions on limbo and purgatory found in appendices 1 and 2, which we will examine in part 1, chapters 3–5). The opening quotation and title of each chapter will always indicate which question that chapter summarizes; likewise, the section headings within each chapter will indicate which of Thomas's articles is addressed in that section.[3] Additionally, the direct quotations from the *Summa* that appear in each chapter can be found in the question of the Supplement under discussion, unless otherwise indicated in a footnote. Note that Thomas addressed various issues related to the Four Last Things in some of his other books, such as his *Compendium of Theology*[4] and certain biblical commentaries, and we might refer to these at times as well.

Each chapter, I'll begin by noting the amazing thoroughness with which Thomas addresses the question under review. Within each article, he first draws on Scripture and the works of Church Fathers to provide a series of realistic objections to his conclusions. Then, in an "On the contrary ..." passage, he usually cites an authority in agreement with his conclusion. He then provides an "I answer that ..." section in which he explains his own conclusion, and, to finish things off, he replies to each of the objections he identified.

Thomas's approach is very thorough indeed, and in his "Treatise on the Resurrection," each article typically has three and at times as many as *sixteen* objections. I'm pretty sure my readers would have objections of their own were I to provide *all* of these objections and Thomas's replies; therefore, our discussion will sometimes cut to the chase and zoom in on the last lines of Thomas's conclusion, though I may draw on other parts of his argument for context or clarification.

I should note that some of the topics Thomas tackles have been explicitly defined and taught as doctrines of the Catholic

---

[3]   Although based on the corresponding questions and articles of the Supplement, chapter titles and section headings are written in my own words.

[4]   Published by Sophia Institute Press as *Aquinas's Shorter Summa*.

Church. I will try to make this clear by integrating passages from the current *Catechism of the Catholic Church* whenever possible. I should note as well that the *Catechism* cites Thomas's writings in abundance.

Last Thoughts

Thomas has given us such a vast number of lasting thoughts about the Four Last Things that I hope and pray that you, dear reader, will be awed, amazed, and inspired as you discover what Thomas wrote about the wondrous things God has in store for us. Still, while Thomas gave us *lasting words*, he did not claim to give us the *last word* on the Four Last Things, since he knew God would continue to bless His Church with new saintly teachers until the end of time.

Therefore, while each of our chapters will stretch our understanding as we contemplate the awesome mysteries that St. Thomas illuminates, each of this book's four parts will end with a "Last Thoughts" chapter, in which we will reflect on the spiritual lessons contained within the preceding chapters, sometimes with the help of the great saints who came after Thomas.

Now that we have dealt with the first things of this book, we must get down to business and invite the Angelic Doctor to guide us on a celestial tour of the four most important things of all—the Four Last Things.

Part 1

Matters of Death and Life

For if man had no hope of another, better life after death,
without doubt death would be very dreadful, and man would
commit any wicked deed rather than taste death. But since
we believe that there is another, better life to which we shall
come after death, it is evident that no one should fear death
or do anything wrong through fear of death: "That through
death He might destroy him who had the empire of death
(that is to say, the Devil) and might deliver them who through
fear of death were all their lifetime subject to servitude."

—*The Aquinas Catechism*[5] (citing Heb. 2:14, 15)

---

[5] Saint Thomas Aquinas, *The Aquinas Catechism: A Simple Explanation of the Catholic Faith by the Church's Greatest Theologian* (Manchester, NH: Sophia Institute Press, 2000), 90.

1

Where Our Souls Go When We Die

The empyrean heaven is a corporeal place, and yet as
soon as it was made it was filled with the holy angels,
as Bede[6] . . . says. Since then angels even as separated
souls are incorporeal, it would seem that some place
should also be assigned to receive separated souls.

—ST, Supplement, 69, 1

Did God create places to receive our souls after death?
The *Catechism* teaches that after death and before the resurrection, our souls are separated from our bodies (1005, 1016). Even in Thomas's time, some people argued that because departed souls are entirely spiritual and do not have material bodies that could be placed in or affected by a physical location, there must not be a place appointed to receive our souls after death. Thomas responds to the contrary. As we see in our opening quotation, "the empyrean heaven,"[7] is a corporeal (material, physical, tangible)

---

[6] St. Bede the Venerable (632–735), *On Genesis*, bk. 1, 2.
[7] "Empyrean" refers to heaven, the sky, or the highest place in the heavens. The Latin term Thomas uses is *caelum empyreum*.

place that is full of angels, which are purely spiritual, bodiless[8] beings. Further, within his *Dialogues*, Pope St. Gregory the Great (540–604) wrote about certain departed souls who were seen or revealed to be in particular places on earth or in hell.

Thomas explains that it is fitting for nobler spiritual substances to be assigned to nobler places, *in the special sense that spiritual substances can be in a place*. The nobler the spiritual substance, the closer it draws to the first substance, which resides in the highest place. That first and noblest substance is God, and while He is everywhere in the universe through His essence, presence, and power,[9] Scripture tells us *His throne is in heaven* (Ps. 103 [102]:19; Isa. 66:1).

Thomas notes that incorporeal spiritual substances, such as a disembodied soul, do not occupy a place in the same way bodies do, but in a special manner unique to spiritual substances—a manner that we, as ensouled bodies here on earth, cannot clearly comprehend. Earlier in the *Summa*, in his "Treatise on the Angels," Thomas explained that angels are immaterial, like our separated souls, but they too *can occupy places*, although they *are not contained by them*. This is akin to the way in which, during life on earth, "the soul is in the body as containing it, not as contained by it."[10]

Further, things can share something in common in two ways: first, *by having the same quality*, as hot things have their heat in

---

8   Thomas notes, however, that angels can *assume* bodies at times to fulfill special missions from God. See *ST* I, 52, 1.

9   "God is in all things by His power, inasmuch as all things are subject to His power: He is by His presence in all things, as all things are bare and open to His eyes: He is in all things by His essence, inasmuch as He is present to all as the cause of their being" (*ST*, I, 8, 3).

10 *ST*, I, 52, 1.

common. Spiritual substances cannot have anything in common with corporeal things in this way. Second, things can share something in common by a kind of *proportionality*, as when the Scriptures *metaphorically* describe the spiritual world in terms of corporeal things. For example, God is spoken of as the sun, because "He is the principle of spiritual life as the sun is of corporeal life" on earth. In this analogical sense, we can see that souls hold things in common with certain places—"for instance, souls that are spiritually enlightened, with luminous bodies, and souls that are plunged in darkness by sin, with dark places."[11]

Finally, separated souls are not affected directly by corporeal places as bodies are, but knowing the places to which they have been appointed brings these souls *joy* or *sorrow*, depending on where they've been placed. This joy or sorrow is part of their reward or punishment, respectively.

Do our souls go straight to heaven or hell when we die?
Some have argued that according to Matthew 25:31–46, souls are not sent to experience the joys of heaven or the torments of hell until *after* the Last Judgment at the end of time.

In response, Thomas again turns to Gregory, who observed in his *Dialogues* that the Last Judgment will indeed provide *further* reward to souls in heaven because "'whereas now they enjoy only the happiness of the soul, afterwards they will enjoy also that of the body, so as to rejoice also in the flesh wherein they bore sorrow and torments for the Lord.' The same is to be said in reference to the damned."

---

[11] *ST*, Supplement, 69, 1.

Thomas makes clear that some souls do go straight to heaven or hell. St. Paul has told us, "For we know that if the earthly tent we live in is destroyed, we have a building from God, a house not made with hands, eternal in the heavens" (2 Cor. 5:1).[12] "Therefore," says Thomas, "after the body's dissolution, the soul has an abode, which has been reserved for it in heaven." Paul also proclaimed, "My desire is to depart and be with Christ" (Phil. 1:23). Since it is a truth of the Faith that Christ is in heaven, Gregory argues that "it cannot be denied that Paul's soul is in heaven likewise." Further, Scripture clearly tells us that some souls do go to hell immediately after death, as was the case for the rich man who died, was buried, and went to hell (Luke 16:22–23).

Still, some souls do not go straight to heaven or hell. Interestingly, Thomas compares the effect of sin on souls after death to that of gravity on physical bodies. Objects lighter than air will immediately rise, while heavier bodies will immediately fall, unless some obstacle impedes their path. A soul that is freed from all debt of sin will rise immediately to heaven, as a soul mired in

[12] In this book, I generally use the Revised Standard Version, Catholic Edition (RSVCE) of the Bible. Thomas used a Bible based on the Latin Vulgate, and in the English translations of the ST that I use, passages from Scripture generally use similar wording to the Douay-Rheims version of the Bible. The words and meanings are usually pretty similar between the Vulgate and the RSVCE, but in some cases, one may find differences in book titles (for example, Ecclesiasticus in the Latin versus Sirach in the RSVCE), chapter numbers (primarily in the Psalms), and verse numbers. I typically point out these differences in footnotes. Further, when it seemed best to me to provide a direct quotation from the ST that contained a reference to Scripture, I used double quotation marks to start and end the passage from the ST, within which single quotation marks demarcate the scriptural passages as they appear in the ST.

mortal sin will descend into hell.[13] An obstacle that can prevent a soul free of mortal sin from rising to heaven is the debt of venial sin, "for which [the soul's] flight must needs be delayed, until the soul is first of all cleansed."[14]

In accord with Thomas, the *Catechism* teaches that after death, we all will face an immediate "particular judgment," in which Christ determines whether our souls will proceed immediately to heaven or hell or first undergo a period of purification (1022).[15]

Are souls ever allowed to leave heaven or hell?

Some passages in Scripture seem to suggest that souls can never leave heaven or hell. For example: "That I may dwell in the

---

[13] The word "mortal," as in "mortal sin," comes from the Latin word *mors*, meaning "death." Mortal sins cause spiritual death and cut us off from God's graces, leading to damnation, and not salvation, if we remain unrepentant. Committing a mortal sin means deliberately and selfishly turning away from God in favor of worldly goods. We read in the *Catechism* that three things are required for a sin to be mortal: "Mortal sin is sin whose object is grave matter and which is also committed with full knowledge and deliberate consent" (1857). Venial sins (from the Latin word *venia*, meaning "pardonable") are smaller moral transgressions regarding less serious matters. They do involve an inordinate or inappropriate focus on worldly goods, but do not entail a deliberate turning away from God. They do not cut us off from God's graces, but "by venial sins man's affections are clogged, so that they are slow in tending towards God" (*ST*, III, 87, 1). Repeated venial sins may also plant the seeds of vicious habits in which mortal sins can take root.

[14] We will thoroughly address this place of cleansing in chapters 3 and 4.

[15] We will discuss particular judgment and the Last Judgment in part 2 of this book.

house of the Lord all the days of my life" (Ps. 27 [26]:4) and "As the cloud fades and vanishes, so he who goes down to Sheol does not come up" (Job 7:9).

To the contrary, Thomas cites the eloquent argument made by St. Jerome (A.D. 347–420) in the following rhetorical questions: "Wouldst thou then lay down the law for God? Wouldst thou put the apostles in chains, imprison them until the day of judgment, and forbid them to be with their lord, them of whom it is written: They follow the Lamb whithersoever He goeth? And if the Lamb is everywhere, therefore we must believe that those also who are with Him are everywhere." Jerome further argues that since demons and the devil wander about the world,[16] "why should the martyrs, after shedding their blood, be imprisoned and unable to go forth?" Thomas also notes that Gregory cited many cases in which the dead have appeared on earth.

Therefore, Thomas concludes that both the good and the wicked are permitted at times to leave their abode. Scripture tells us that no one leaves heaven or hell "simply" or forever, but it does not tell us that souls cannot sometimes leave their abodes for limited periods of time to take part in the affairs of the living and appear to men "according to Divine providence," as Thomas says.

What are the "limbo of hell" and "Abraham's bosom," and are they the same thing?

We proclaim in the Creed that Christ "descended into hell." The *Catechism* explains that "Jesus, like all men, experienced death

---

[16] Perhaps this brings immediately to mind the words "seeking the ruin of souls" from the Prayer to St. Michael, the Archangel.

and in his soul joined the others in the realm of the dead. But he descended there as Savior, proclaiming the Good News to the spirits imprisoned there" (632). Further, "Scripture calls the abode of the dead, to which the dead Christ went down, 'hell'—*Sheol* in Hebrew or *Hades* in Greek—because those who are there are deprived of the vision of God" (CCC 633).

With this context in mind, let us now go to Thomas. He argues that after death, souls cannot find rest except through faith, as Hebrews 11:6 says: "For whoever would draw near to God must believe that he exists and that he rewards those who seek him." Because Abraham was "the first to sever himself from the body of unbelievers, and to receive a special sign of faith," the place of rest given to people after death is called "Abraham's bosom," as we see in Luke 16:22–23, which says that the unfaithful rich man Dives[17] was damned to Hades, and the faithful Lazarus "was carried by the angels to Abraham's bosom." Before Christ came and set their souls free, the faithful in hell experienced partial rest in that they were not punished, but their ultimate end—being with God in heaven—had not yet been fulfilled. So the same place is called the "limbo of hell" because it was a place of waiting "in limbo" where souls were deprived of their final rest in God, and "Abraham's bosom" because of the partial rest it afforded before the coming of Christ. "The state of the holy Fathers as regards what was good in it was called Abraham's bosom, but as regards its deficiencies it was called hell."

Since the coming of Christ, Abraham's bosom is no longer called the limbo of hell, because the saints in Abraham's bosom

---

[17] The passage speaks of a "rich man," who has traditionally been called Dives after the Latin for "rich" or "wealthy."

now have complete rest in that they do see God. It is in this sense that the Church prays, echoing St. Luke, that departed souls will be carried to Abraham's bosom.

Is limbo the same as the hell of the damned?

Thomas states quite succinctly that "in hell, there is no redemption [Office of the Dead, resp. vii]. But the saints [the Patriarchs, or Fathers, and the other faithful who departed before Christ] were redeemed from limbo. Therefore, limbo is not the same as hell." Limbo was a temporary place of waiting qualitatively distinct from the hell of the damned. Still, Thomas notes that hell and limbo may occupy the same place, or may be continuous such that some higher part of hell contains limbo.

Is the limbo of children the same as the limbo of the Fathers?

The limbo of children is the abode of children who die without Baptism. Because their souls still bear the stain of Original Sin, they cannot experience the Beatific Vision of God in heaven, though they receive no other kind of punishment.

Thomas argues that an arrangement similar to the one described in the previous section may exist between the "limbo of children" and the "limbo of the Fathers," in that the two may occupy the same place, while the limbo of the Fathers may occupy a higher part. One reason is that unbaptized children "have no hope of the blessed life, as the Fathers in limbo had, in whom, moreover, shone forth the light of faith and grace." The faithful who died before the coming of Christ waited in the limbo of the Fathers until, set free by Christ, they saw God face-to-face in heaven. The children in limbo, on the other hand, still bear the stain of Original Sin, and thus will never reach heaven (but they remain beloved by God, and will enjoy *natural* happiness for eternity).[18]

Should there be so many resting places for souls?

Sometimes, non-Catholic Christians criticize the Church's teaching on the various resting places for souls. They think *heaven* and *hell*, the last two of the Last Things, suffice, and any other resting places derive from merely the traditions of men. Indeed, even before the Reformation, and within the Catholic Church herself, there were many misgivings and misunderstandings regarding the resting places for souls. Some people held that there should be many *more* resting places, even an *infinite* number, since the degrees of merit and sin are infinite!

That Thomas provides and replies to a full *ten objections* in question 69, article 7, "Whether So Many Abodes Should Be Distinguished?" demonstrates the extent of this controversy. I invite you to read these objections and his replies at your leisure, but for now, I'll supply a few of Thomas's main conclusions.

Thomas notes that "the abodes of souls are distinguished according to the souls' various states." While on earth, united to the body, the soul is "in the state of meriting," but after death, separated from the body, the soul can only receive good or evil for the merits it has already acquired, although it may not be in

---

[18] We will examine the limbo of children more fully in chapter 5, "On God's Love for Unbaptized Souls." In that chapter, we will also address CCC 1261, which summarizes Church teaching on children who die without Baptism.

the proper state to do so. If it is, the soul will receive its final reward according to the two ways Thomas identifies. If the soul is pure and good, its abode is paradise, or *heaven*. If the soul is evil in terms of actual sin, its abode is *hell*, while if the soul is evil in terms of Original Sin only, its abode is the *limbo of children*. On the other hand, if by sin the soul is hindered or delayed from receiving its final reward, the soul's abode is either *purgatory* (if the soul is hindered by a defect of the person, that is, personal venial sins) or *the limbo of the Fathers*, that is, Abraham's bosom (if the soul is hindered by a defect of nature, namely, the guilt of human nature that had not yet been expiated by Christ).

2

The State of Our Souls after Death

I answer that, There are many opinions on this question.

—ST, Supplement, 70, 1

Do our souls still have powers of sensation after death?

Shortly after my mother's death, an adult family member told one of our young sons that she was watching over him from heaven. He responded with a question: "Can Grandma see through our roof?"

As our opening quotation makes clear, in Thomas's day, the question of whether we retain our capacities of sensation before our bodies are reunited with our souls was quite the contentious issue. Indeed, when addressing this topic in question 70, article 1, Thomas presents and replies to a full seven objections to his own reasoned opinion. Thomas's conclusions are based on his extensive treatment of the nature and powers of the human soul, which he built upon the work of Aristotle (384–322 B.C.) and presented in the First Part of the great *Summa*. And what were his conclusions?

To make this complicated story short, Thomas notes that some of the powers of the human soul are rooted in bodily operations and cannot be exercised "except through the medium of the body." There can be no sight without eyes, hearing without ears, feeling without skin, smell without the nose, or taste without the tongue—along with, of course, the areas of the brain to which these organs are connected. For this reason, while the soul is separated from the body, we cannot take in new sensory information. Thomas would argue that if Grandma were in heaven, she would in fact be *unable* to see singular things, such as her grandson, through the normal operations of the senses and intellect. Still, there is another "way of understanding … by the infusion of species by God, and in that way it is possible for the intellect to know singulars,"[19] should it be God's will. If God desires that Grandma see her grandchild at some particular time for some particular reason, He will be fully capable of bestowing such knowledge upon her soul.

At the same time, Thomas agrees with St. Augustine (A.D. 354–430) that the separated soul "clings keenly to its senses and wits." In other words, our powers of sensation can be said to remain in our separated souls in a restricted, *virtual sense*, in that our souls will regain the ability to exercise these powers immediately upon reunion with our bodies at the resurrection.

Further, the soul also possesses some powers that "are performed by the soul without a bodily organ—for instance, to understand, to consider, [and] to will." These "intellectual" powers of the soul (as contrasted with its "vegetative" and "sensitive" powers) will not be diminished by the corruption of bodily organs and will therefore remain in separated souls.[20]

---

[19] *ST*, I, 89, 4.

[20] In brief, the human soul's *vegetative powers*, which we share with plant and lower animal life, are nourishment, growth, and

Can the separated soul perform acts of the sensitive powers such as memory?

Once again, we are grateful for Thomas's guidance as we consider this complicated question! He presents five objections, buttressed by passages from Augustine[21] and Aristotle, that seem to suggest

---

reproduction. The *sensitive powers*, which we share with lower animals, include the powers of locomotion (self-movement), sensation, and appetites toward desirable things and away from undesirable things. In addition to external senses, such as vision, hearing, and the like, humans and some animals also possess "internal" sensory powers, including imagination; the common sense, which integrates data from the various external senses; memory; and the estimative sense, which determines whether what is perceived by our senses is helpful or harmful to us. We also possess appetites by which we naturally desire what we perceive to be good for us and avoid what we perceive to be harmful.

Of all creatures on earth, humans alone possess the *intellectual powers*—intellect and will—whereby we can understand things on an abstract, conceptual, universal level, rather than a merely particular level; communicate through language; and guide our own appetites and behaviors by reason and the power of the will, rather than mere instinct or training, as with the lower animals. These intellectual powers are immaterial and spiritual. They reflect that we are made in the image and likeness of God. Further, in humans alone, the intellectual powers can guide and shape the operations of the internal senses.

For more details on the powers of the soul, see *ST*, I, 75–79; Thomas's *Commentary on Aristotle's De Anima*; or the summaries provided in my books *Unearthing Your Ten Talents, The One-Minute Aquinas*, or *How to Think Like Aquinas*. For more on these powers as exercised by separated souls, see the eight articles of *ST*, I, 89, "On the Knowledge of the Separated Soul."

[21] Quite interestingly, Thomas notes that the work of Augustine (*On the Spirit and Soul*) cited in one objection may not actually be Augustine's. Some have argued that a Cistercian compiled

that separated souls will be able to perform acts of the sensitive powers such as imagination, memory, and the concupiscible and irascible appetites.[22]

In his argument to the contrary, Thomas ascribes to Plato (ca. 428–348 B.C.) some of the confusion over the powers of the separated soul. Plato understood the soul as a perfect substance independent of the body, which is merely the soul's instrument. When the soul exercises its powers, it acts first upon itself, and then upon the body. For example, the act of seeing originates within the soul, which first moves itself in order to move the eyes, through which it exercises the power of sight.

Contrary to Plato, Aristotle reasoned that the sensitive powers are exercised by a *composite* of soul and body. Thomas would agree with Aristotle that *your soul* is not reading this book; *you*, as a composite of body and soul, are reading it. Take away your eyes, and your soul cannot read a single word! (And, of course, neither can your eyes read it without the powers of your soul!)

In other words, when separated from the body, souls cannot exercise their sensitive powers, including the kind of sensitive memory whereby we remember specific events in the past, as well as the concupiscible appetite of desire, the irascible appetite of aversion, and the passions that flow from them, such as love, joy, sorrow, and the like. Still, the immaterial soul *will* be able to exercise its higher, intellectual, uniquely human powers. These include the intellectual powers of memory that abstract from all differences of time, retaining universal concepts; and

---

it from the works of Augustine and several other authors, even adding some of his own ideas!

[22] The concupiscible appetite moves us to desire the good, while the irascible appetite motivates us to avoid or overcome obstacles to the good.

the passions (such as those named above) that derive not from the sensitive appetites, but from acts of the will, which is in the intellectual part of the soul.

Can a separated soul suffer from physical fire?

Responding to passages from Augustine, Gregory, and Aristotle that suggest separated souls cannot suffer from physical fire, Thomas takes Christ Himself as his main source. He cites the words Christ will proclaim to the damned on Judgment Day: "Depart from me, you cursed, into the eternal fire prepared for the devil and his angels" (Matt. 25:41). Christ made it clear that demons, who lack physical bodies, suffer from fire in hell. Therefore, the same must be possible for separated souls. Further, there is a kind of fittingness to the punishment. Since in sinning the soul makes itself subject to the body, "it is just that it should be punished by being made subject to a bodily thing by suffering therefrom."

Citing Augustine, Gregory, Bishop Julian of Toledo (642–690), and "the Master" (Peter Lombard), Thomas elaborates that lacking a body, the soul is not corrupted or destroyed by the physical fire, but as the soul is held by the body during life, so the soul is imprisoned by the flames of hell. In Thomas's words: "The corporeal fire is enabled as the instrument of the vengeance of Divine justice thus to detain a spirit; and thus it has a penal effect on it, by hindering it from fulfilling its own will, that is by hindering it from acting where it will and as it will."

3

On the Nature and Purpose of Purgatory

Those who deny Purgatory speak against the justice of God.

—ST, Supplement, Appendix 2, 1

Does purgatory exist?

Some who deny the existence of purgatory cite Revelation 14:13: "Blessed are the dead who die in the Lord henceforth. 'Blessed indeed,' says the Spirit, 'that they may rest from their labors, for their deeds follow them!'" The *Catechism* makes it clear, however, that purgatory exists as a place of cleansing or purgation (1030–1032). Thomas explains that the verse from Revelation refers to *the labor of working to gain spiritual merit*, but does *not* address *the labor of suffering to be cleansed from sin*. Any person whose soul is in purgatory has died in charity and merits the eternal reward of heaven, but only *after* having been cleansed of any remaining venial sins. A soul in purgatory may also bear the effects of mortal sins that have been forgiven, but for which the person has not yet made satisfaction through penance. Revelation confirms that "nothing unclean shall enter" heaven (21:27).

Thomas further explains Church teaching on purgatory with another passage from Scripture and a line from the Eastern

Church Father St. Gregory of Nyssa (A.D. 335–394). Scripture tells us, in reference to Judah Maccabee, that "it was a holy and pious thought" that "he made atonement for the dead, that they might be delivered from their sin" (2 Macc. 12:45).[23] Thomas elaborates that there is no need to pray for the souls in heaven, since they already have their reward. Neither is a need to pray for those in hell, because they can no longer be freed from their sins. Yet those who have died in charity can never suffer everlasting death, since charity covers all sins (Prov. 10:12), and those who follow Christ will have eternal life (John 11:26). Gregory of Nyssa says that the person who loves and believes in Christ, but dies before his sins have been washed away, "is set free after death by the fire of Purgatory."

Here, God's justice is made clear. He has provided the purging fires of purgatory so that believers who die still tainted by sin may become clean in the afterlife. Further, He has provided a means whereby we, through our prayers as the Church Militant on earth, may help loosen the bonds of sin of the Church Suffering in purgatory, so that they might sooner rest eternally with God in heaven. Such prayer is, indeed, "a holy and pious thing."

---

[23] We should note that First and Second Maccabees were among the seven books removed from the canon of the Old Testament by Luther and other early reformers in the 1500s. These books are referred to as the "Apocrypha" (meaning "doubtful") by Protestants and as the "Deuterocanonical" (meaning "second canon") books by Catholics. Protestants do not consider these books the inspired Word of God, though St. Thomas and the Church Fathers and Doctors before and after him did. The Catholic Church has always recognized them as divinely inspired, since the Old Testament canon was established by that selfsame Church. For a list of all seventy-three books of the Bible, see CCC 120.

Are souls cleansed and damned within the same place?

While the existence of purgatory is an established doctrine of the Church, made clear especially at the Councils of Florence and Trent (CCC 1031), Thomas tells us that "nothing is clearly stated in Scripture about the situation of Purgatory, nor is it possible to offer convincing arguments on this question." In other words, the Bible does not tell us exactly *where* purgatory is. Still, Thomas declares that some opinions are "of no account"—for example, the idea that purgatory is somewhere above us because the state of the souls in purgatory lies between those living on earth and God in heaven. Nonsense, says Thomas, since those souls are not punished for being above us, "but for that which is lowest in them, namely sin."

Thomas notes that it is "probable," according to statements made by holy men and many private revelations, that "there is a twofold place of Purgatory." One place is according to the "common law." This place is below us and near hell, so the same fire torments both the souls being cleansed and the souls that are damned in hell, though the damned, being of lower merit, are consigned to the lowest place. Thomas makes the important distinction that while the fires of hell serve to *afflict* the damned, the fires of purgatory, while painful, serve primarily to *cleanse* souls from sin.

The second place of purgatory is according to a special "dispensation," whereby, "as we read,"[24] souls are sometimes punished

---

[24] We can find evidence of this dispensation in the many stories of people who have interacted with suffering souls or received private revelations of purgatory. For a powerful text chronicling such revelations, see Fr. F. X. Schouppe, S.J., *Purgatory: Explained by the Lives and Legends of the Saints* (London: Burns and Oates, 1893; Rockford, IL: TAN Books, 1993).

in various places so that the living may learn from them, or those souls themselves may be "succored [comforted], seeing that their punishment being made known to the living may be mitigated through the prayers of the Church."

Indeed, we can all hope that we will never know firsthand where in hell the damned reside, and that, should we come to know purgatory's location (or locations) firsthand, we will not reside there very long!

4

On the State of the Souls in Purgatory

*In Purgatory there will be a twofold pain; one will be the pain of
loss, namely the delay of the divine vision, and the pain of sense,
namely punishment by corporeal fire. With regard to both the
least pain of Purgatory surpasses the greatest pain of this life.*

—ST, Supplement, Appendix 1, 2, 1

Are the pains of purgatory greater than any pains of this life?

In this chapter's opening quotation, Thomas expands upon Augustine's declaration that "this fire of Purgatory will be more severe than any pain that can be felt, seen, or conceived in this world." The soul's *pain of losing* the divine vision of God will be greater than any sense of loss of earth because the more we desire something, the more we suffer when it is absent. (Any person who has lost a loved one can attest to this kind of pain.) Yet *in purgatory, our overwhelming desire to see God is completely undiluted.* The soul's desire is not hindered or distracted by things of the body. Further, the soul knows that had it not been held back by the weight of sin, it would already have achieved the "Sovereign Good," as Thomas puts it. Therefore, the soul grieves most intensely because the delay of purgatory keeps it from its ultimate goal.

The soul's *pain of sense* in purgatory does not refer to a hurt or injury itself, but to the *sense* thereof. "The more sensitive a thing is," Thomas explains, "the greater the pain caused by that which hurt it." We know from experience that hurts inflicted upon the most sensitive parts of our body cause the greatest pain. Because all bodily sensations arise from the soul, it follows that the most exquisite pain is suffered when the soul itself is hurt.

Therefore, Thomas concludes that the pains of purgatory, both of loss and of sense, surpass all the pains we experience during life.

Do souls in purgatory suffer their punishment voluntarily?

This is an interesting question with, perhaps, a surprising answer, for we cannot imagine *choosing* to suffer such great pain. Evidence suggesting the answer is no includes the anecdotes in Gregory's *Dialogues* about souls in purgatory who appear to the living and ask to be set free. Thomas says the answer is yes, but this requires precise thinking about just what makes an act voluntary.

First, an act may be voluntary as an *absolute* act of the will. In this sense, the very idea of punishment is contrary to the nature of the will, which always seeks the good, and not pain or punishment. Second, an act may be voluntary as a *conditional* act of the will, as when a person willingly undergoes some pain or punishment because it allows him to obtain a good he could not attain otherwise. Thomas provides the simple example of submitting to painful surgical procedures to restore our health and the extreme example of martyrs, who submit to bodily death to procure their reward in heaven. It is in this second sense that the punishments in purgatory are voluntary, since the souls know they will someday be set free and obtain their goal of heaven. This we see in the many stories of souls in purgatory who appear to people on earth and ask for prayers to hasten their purification.

Do demons punish the souls in purgatory?

Building on a statement of "the Master," Peter Lombard, that "they will have for torturers in their pains, those who were their tempters in sin," some have argued that demons torment the souls in purgatory. Thomas, however, notes that it would be contrary to justice for someone who has triumphed over someone else to be subjected to him after the victory. Any souls who attain purgatory have triumphed over the temptations that would have left them in mortal sin at death, and will not be subjected to their tempters. Triumphant souls with remaining venial sins will not be punished by demons, but will be purified in purgatory by divine justice alone.

Do the pains of purgatory atone for the guilt of venial sins?

To show that the pains of purgatory cannot atone for the *guilt* of venial sins, some cite a gloss[25] on the verse "There is sin which is mortal" (1 John 5:16). According to this gloss, "it is vain to ask pardon after death for what was not amended in this life." Indeed, Thomas supplies five objections to the idea that the guilt of venial sins is expiated (atoned for) in the fires of purgatory. He responds

[25] The *Glossa Ordinaria*, widely used in the Middle Ages, was a version of the Latin Vulgate whose margins contained brief glosses (comments or explanations) compiled from the writings of various Church Fathers.

by building on the opinions of both Gregory and Augustine that "certain slight sins will be remitted in the life to come."

Thomas reminds us (expanding on 1 John 5:16–17) that some sins are mortal and some are merely venial. These venial sins are the "wood, hay, [or] straw" that is cleansed and consumed by the fire of purgatory (1 Cor. 3:12). The punishments of purgatory cleanse us of the *debt of punishment* for mortal sins that have been confessed and whose *guilt* has been forgiven, but for which we did not make satisfaction while on earth. Regarding venial sins, Thomas makes clear that we should never become complacent and uncaring about our venial sins, as complete complacency and lack of contrition could lead to mortal sin. Still, for venial sins, the punishments of purgatory can cleanse not only their *debt of punishment*, but also their *guilt*.

We can see this in the case of a person in a state of grace, with no mortal sin on his soul, who dies in his sleep after committing some venial sin for which he has not yet experienced contrition. Indeed, in a fascinating hypothetical example (one that perhaps reveals our Angelic Doctor's penchant for lofty and abstract thought!), Thomas describes the case of a man who commits some venial sin and "has no actual thought of being forgiven or of remaining in that sin, but thinks perhaps about a triangle having its three angles equal to two right angles, and while engaged in this thought falls asleep, and dies." Thomas declares that such a man would be cleansed from the guilt of his venial sin in the fires of purgatory after death, "because this punishment so far as it is voluntary, will have the power, by virtue of grace, to expiate all such guilt as is compatible with grace."[26]

---

[26] The New Advent online *Summa Theologica* provides an additional note here from Thomas's book *On Evil* (*De Malo*) on

(How powerful and generous are the graces Christ has given us by conquering sin through His death on the Cross and healing us with His loving charity!)

Does the fire of purgatory pay the debt of punishment for sin?

Thomas notes that as the punishment one voluntarily endures *in this life* serves as satisfaction to atone the guilt of sin, all the more so will the more grievous pains of purgatory atone for the debt of punishment for sins. Anyone in debt is freed by paying what he owes. The obligation incurred by guilt is the debt of punishment, and a person is freed from that obligation by undergoing the punishment. Therefore, the answer is *yes*: "The punishment of Purgatory cleanses from the debt of punishment."

Are some souls released from purgatory before others?

Some argue that because more-grievous sins warrant more-severe punishments, more-serious sinners would be punished more severely in purgatory, but all souls would suffer for the same amount of time. Thomas answers with an interesting observation about a line from the writings of "the Apostle" (St. Paul) comparing venial sins to wood, straw, and hay (1 Cor. 3:12): as wood remains longer in a fire than straw and hay, some kinds of venial sins will be punished longer than others in the fires of purgatory. Some

---

this rather complicated issue: "St. Thomas expresses himself differently, De Malo, 7, 2, ad 9,17: 'Guilt is not remitted by punishment, but venial sin as to its guilt is remitted in Purgatory by virtue of grace, not only as existing in the habit, but as proceeding to the act of charity in detestation of venial sin.'" https://www.newadvent.org/summa/6002.htm#article4

venial sins "cling" to us more persistently than do others, as we are more inclined to indulge in them repeatedly, and "since that which clings more persistently is more slowly cleansed, it follows that some are tormented in Purgatory longer than others, for as much as their affections were steeped in venial sins." Further, the *severity* of punishment corresponds to the amount of guilt, while the *length* corresponds to how firmly the sin has taken root in the soul. Therefore, some souls may spend longer in purgatory, but suffer less, and vice versa.

5

On God's Love for Unbaptized Souls

*Although unbaptized children are separated from God as regards
the union of glory, they are not utterly separated from Him: in fact
they are united to Him by their share of natural goods, and so will
also be able to rejoice in Him by their natural knowledge and love.*

—ST, Supplement, Appendix 1, 1, 2

*Do souls who die with only Original Sin
suffer from bodily fires?*

This is a very difficult and serious issue, especially as it regards
infants who die without Baptism. Paragraph 1252 of the *Catechism* explains that Baptism is an "immemorial tradition of the
Church," dating back to the time of the apostles when entire
"households," quite possibly including infants, were baptized (see
Acts 16:15, 33; 18:8; 1 Cor. 1:16). It is the sacrament of faith
that Christ Himself affirms is necessary for salvation (CCC 1257,
citing John 3:5). By Baptism, "*all sins* are forgiven, original sin
and all personal sins, as well as all punishment for sin" (CCC
1263, italics original). For this reason, the Church declares it
urgent that we do not "prevent little children coming to Christ
through the gift of holy Baptism" (CCC 1261). In light of these

basic teachings, we turn now to Thomas's treatment of the state of unbaptized souls who die with Original Sin only.

Citing Augustine's claim that "children who depart this life without the sacrament of Baptism will be punished everlastingly,"[27] some have argued that such children, like the souls in purgatory and the souls of the damned, will be punished by fire. Thomas condemns this sorry error, beginning his argument with Augustine's statement that those who die with only Original Sin will suffer the lightest punishment of all. Clearly, these souls will not suffer the most-grievous pains of hell. Further, "the grief of sensible punishment corresponds to the pleasure of sin (Apocalypse 18:7) … but there is no pleasure in original sin," so it does not warrant eternal fire.

Thomas also cites the Eastern Church Father St. Gregory Nazianzen (A.D. 329–390), who wrote that there are three classes of unbaptized people:

1. those who refuse Baptism
2. those who have put it off until the end of life, but are surprised by death
3. those who failed to receive it through no fault of their own

---

[27] From *De Fide ad Petrum*, 27. In Thomas's day, *De Fide ad Petrum* was attributed to Augustine. It is now attributed to Fulgentius of Ruspe (ca. A.D. 460–533), who lived about a century after Augustine.

In any case, of all the Doctors of the Church, Augustine examined the nature of Original Sin most clearly. He was not, however, the first to discuss the doctrine. St. Irenaeus of Lyon (ca. A.D. 130–202), for example, alluded to it, as did the inspired writers of Scripture. See Romans 5:12–21 and 1 Corinthians 15:21–22, which refer to the spreading of sin to all men through Adam's sin, and Psalm 51 [50]:5, which says, "Behold, I was brought forth in iniquity, and in sin did my mother conceive me."

The first, he says, will be punished for all their sins, including their contempt for Baptism. The second will be punished, though less severely, for their neglect. As for the third, however, a just judge would consign them neither to a heavenly reward nor to an infernal punishment, since "they are without wickedness and malice, and have suffered rather than caused their loss of Baptism."

Thomas answers that punishment should be proportionate to fault, citing Isaiah 27:8, which says that God contends with sinners "measure by measure." The punishment due a person whose nature has not been cleansed of Original Sin is simply the lack of the necessary grace to attain the divine vision of God, and this alone is sufficient punishment. Human nature alone cannot attain the Beatific Vision, but these souls "will suffer no loss whatever in other kinds of perfection and goodness which are consequent upon human nature by virtue of its principles."

Do unbaptized souls suffer spiritually because of their state?
Having concluded that the unbaptized souls of children will suffer no sensible punishment, Thomas now addresses whether they will suffer "spiritual affliction." Here, he offers additional sublime and comforting insights and concludes that their souls will *not* suffer spiritually either.

Thomas begins with five objections holding that unbaptized souls will suffer spiritual pain. One of the most striking arguments builds upon a comment of St. John Chrysostom (ca. A.D. 347–407) indicating that the loss of the Beatific Vision is more painful than hellfire. Since unbaptized souls will be deprived of seeing God, they will experience great spiritual affliction. Thomas responds to this objection by clarifying that the pain of losing the

Beatific Vision will afflict those who are damned for their *actual sins*, because they know they could have obtained eternal life with God, but instead turned away from Him. Children will *not* suffer from this deprivation, because they were unable to obtain the Beatific Vision, and did not lose it through their own actions.

Quite interestingly, Thomas draws on the insights of the Stoic philosopher Seneca the Younger (ca. 4 B.C.–A.D. 65), who wrote that a wise person is not disturbed by things he cannot control. Thomas expounds that one guided by right reason does not grieve over something beyond his power to attain, but only over things he has the power to attain. "Thus no wise man grieves for being unable to fly like a bird, or for that he is not a king or an emperor, since these things are not due to him." Thomas proceeds to explain that the souls of unbaptized children will not grieve for their lack of the divine vision, but they will "rejoice for that they will have a large share of God's goodness and their own natural perfections."

Further, Thomas concludes, "Although unbaptized children are separated from God as regards the union of glory, they are not utterly separated from Him: in fact they are united to Him by their share of natural goods, and so will also be able to rejoice in Him by their natural knowledge and love." Clearly, then, Catholic teaching on the state of unbaptized souls is not so harsh a doctrine as some might assume.

As for our modern *Catechism*, the word "limbo" does not appear in the text. While we are reminded of the "urgency" of providing "the gift of holy Baptism" for little children, "the Church can only entrust them [the unbaptized] to the mercy of God, as she does in her funeral rites for them." Indeed, we are to recall the love and tenderness of Christ, who desired that the children come to Him (Mark 10:14). This allows us "to hope that there is a way of salvation for children who have died without Baptism" (CCC 1261).

Perhaps this is a case to which we might apply the words of Jerome we encountered in this book's first chapter: "Wouldst thou then lay down the law for God?" We can pray that we will one day know God's answer to the question of how unbaptized children spend eternity.[28]

---

[28] For additional details regarding current Church teaching on this topic, see International Theological Commission, *The Hope of Salvation for Infants Who Die without Being Baptised*, April 19, 2007, http://www.vatican.va/roman_curia/congregations/cfaith/ cti_documents/rc_con_cfaith_doc_20070419_un-baptised -infants_en.html.

6

Why We Should Pray for the Dead

I answer that, Charity, which is the bond uniting the
members of the Church, extends not only to the living, but
also to the dead who die in charity. For charity which is
the life of the soul, even as the soul is the life of the body,
has no end; "Charity never falleth away" (1 Corinthians
13:8). Moreover, the dead live in the memory of the living:
wherefore the intention of the living can be directed to them.

—ST, Supplement, 71, 2

We must consider two issues before we proceed into this fascinating chapter, which reveals the beauty and wisdom of the teachings of the Church and her Angelic Doctor on this important topic—a topic that, sadly, has been considered moot by most non-Catholic Christians since the Reformation.

First, while the title of this chapter emphasizes *prayers* for the dead, Thomas actually used the more general Latin term *suffragia,* translated as "suffrages." This broader term includes not only prayers but also Masses and other pious acts or works performed to assist a person in purgatory. In this chapter, we will use "suffrages" in every question except the second, in which, like Thomas, we will use the word "works" (*operibus* in Latin).

Second, Thomas presents a full fourteen articles, with many dozens of objections and replies, within the Supplement's question 71, "On the Suffrages for the Dead." For the sake of clarity (and charity toward you, dear reader), I will present this chapter's answers as tersely as possible, zooming in on the bottom lines, while suggesting that some time, at your leisure, you explore Thomas's complete treatment of these issues to wonder at and enjoy each line of his arguments.

Can the suffrages of one person profit someone else?

While some argue that the prayers and pious works of one person cannot possibly aid someone else, since we reap what we sow (Gal. 6:8) and God renders to every man according to his works (Ps. 62 [61]:13), Thomas responds that we are companions with all who fear God (Ps. 119 [118]:63). The faithful are united by charity as members of the Church's one body. "Now one member is assisted by another. Therefore one man can be assisted by the merits of another." The communion of saints is an article of faith expressed in the Apostles' Creed. We all benefit from one another's charity and share in each other's merits, so that even in heaven "each one will rejoice in the goods of others." While our prayers or other suffrages cannot directly alter the *state* of a person's soul after death (namely, whether it will be sent to hell, purgatory, or heaven), our prayers and meritorious acts on earth, operating through God's divine power, mercy, and generosity, can help others united in the Faith "either for the fulfillment of satisfaction or for some similar purpose that does not change their state." Our prayers cannot deposit a loved one in heaven, but they may help him, if he is in purgatory, to enter heaven's gates sooner.

Can the works of the living profit the dead?

Here, Thomas cites 2 Maccabees 12:46 (v. 45 in the RSVCE) on the holiness and wholesomeness of prayers for the dead; Augustine on the appropriateness of the priest's prayer for the dead from the altar during Mass; the Eastern Church Doctor St. John Damascene (676–749) on how Christ's holy apostles sanctioned commemorations for the dead; and Dionysius[29] on how the early Church prayed for the dead and taught that suffrages profited them. He then provides the beautiful lines of our chapter's opening quotation on how the members of the Church, both living and dead, are united by the bonds of charity. Indeed, the pious prayers and works of the living profit the dead in purgatory in the same two ways they profit the living: through the aforementioned bond of charity and because the intention of acts of the living can be directed to them. Again, he makes clear that the suffrages of the living cannot change the state of departed souls from unhappiness to happiness, but "they avail for the diminution of punishment or something of the kinds that involves no change in the state of the dead."

---

[29] Author of works including *On the Divine Names* and *The Celestial Hierarchy* and believed in the Middle Ages to be St. Dionysius the Areopagite, who was converted by St. Paul (Acts 17:34). ("Areopagite" refers to a rocky outcrop called the Areopagus — meaning "Ares' rock" in Greek — near the Acropolis in Athens. The Areopagus was the site of St. Paul's famous sermon to the Athenians.) He is usually referred to now as Pseudo-Dionysius or Pseudo-Denys and is believed to be a late fifth- to early sixth-century Syrian Christian theologian and philosopher who wrote under the name of the famous St. Dionysius.

Do the suffrages of sinners profit the dead?

Here we confront the interesting question of whether suffrages performed by people in the state of mortal sin can provide aid to the dead. Thomas says we must consider two ways that suffrages may be performed by the living. The first regards the sacraments. The sacraments have their efficacy in themselves through God's power, regardless of whether the priest who confers them is himself wicked. In that way, the suffrages of the sinner *do* indeed still profit the dead. Secondly, if we consider the deeds of a sinner who offers suffrages as his own act, they are *not* meritorious to him or to anyone else. Still, if we consider a sinner's deeds as representing the whole Church, as when a wicked priest performs a burial service, then the suffrages still profit the dead, though they would provide yet more profit if the person offering the suffrage were also in the state of grace through charity. This is also the case for suffrages performed by a person in the state of mortal sin at the behest of someone in the state of grace.

Do the suffrages of the living for the dead
profit the living who offer them?

In a sermon about "those who fell asleep in the Faith," St. John Damascene declared that just as the priest who anoints a sick man first partakes of the anointing oil himself, so too "whoever strives for his neighbor's salvation first of all profits himself and afterwards his neighbor." Thomas explains that a work of suffrage can be considered in two ways. First, when a work of suffrage is performed to absolve another person from his debt of punishment, it does not absolve the first person's punishment also, since the equality of *justice* requires that the debt of two sinners requires greater satisfaction than that of one. Secondly, however, the suffrage may be considered an act that merits eternal life, because it proceeds from *charity*. As a meritorious act of charity, a suffrage profits not only the person for whom it is done, "but also and still more the doer."

Do suffrages profit the souls in hell?

This was a controversial question in the early Church. Certain stories suggested that prayers and pious acts offered by the living could aid or even free the damned. In *The Lives of the Fathers*, as well as one of St. John Damascene's sermons, we read of Macarius, who found the skull of a dead man on the road. After praying for the man's soul, he learned that the skull had belonged to a pagan priest condemned to hell. Yet the priest came to tell Macarius that he and others were aided by his prayers.

In the same sermon, St. John Damascene reports that St. Gregory Nazianzen, after praying for the deceased Roman emperor Trajan, heard a voice from heaven saying, "I have heard thy voice, and I pardon Trajan." Further, some argued that the damned who had shared the Faith, participated in the sacraments, and performed good works could be released from their punishment with sufficient suffrages on the part of the Church.

Thomas responded that the last opinion was an error deriving from Origen of Alexandria (A.D. 184–253), and the other two incidents should be interpreted very carefully, since the pagan priest's punishment in hell was not diminished; rather, he experienced a temporary and imaginary joy by being allowed to see Macarius. Even the demons, Thomas notes, are said to experience joy when they lead us to sin, though this does not diminish their punishment. As for Trajan, it is possible that he was recalled to life by Gregory's prayers and then received the grace whereby his sins were pardoned. It is also possible that Trajan was not freed from hell, but that his punishment was temporarily suspended until Judgment Day. In either case, these are not in accordance with the general law regarding the effects of suffrages, but are, to paraphrase Augustine, "miracles of the Divine power."

Thomas answers this question in the negative, noting that the souls of the damned have died "cut off from the bond of charity," and cannot be aided by the prayers of the living. They cannot even sense a diminishment of punishment through the knowledge that the living are praying for them, because, as Augustine has noted, the souls in hell cannot see what is happening on earth, barring a special miracle.

Do suffrages profit the souls in purgatory?

The souls in purgatory are precisely those who benefit from the suffrages of the living. Thomas notes that "the punishment of purgatory is intended to supplement the satisfaction which was not fully completed in the body," and since we saw above that the suffrages of one person can aid another, either living or dead, "the suffrages of the living, without any doubt, profit those who are in purgatory." Indeed, we see this confirmed in our *Catechism*, which explains that from the beginning, the Church has offered prayers, especially the Eucharistic sacrifice, in suffrage for the souls in purgatory. Further, "the Church also commends almsgiving, indulgences, and works of penance on behalf of the dead" (CCC 1032). Thomas explains that the efficacy of suffrages proceeds from "the Divine mercy, which transcends human merits."

Do suffrages profit the souls of children in limbo?

Thomas seconds Augustine's conclusion that suffrages cannot aid those who have died "without the faith that works by love," that is, without the graces and theological virtues that flow from the sacrament of Baptism. Here, we might recall Thomas's opinion that the souls of children in limbo are still able to rejoice in God through natural love (though not supernatural charity). We should also keep in mind the hope expressed in the *Catechism* that God *might* hold a way to salvation for children who die without Baptism (1261).

Do suffrages profit the saints in heaven?

To make a moderately long story short: *no*. The saints need no help reaching heaven, since they are already there! As Thomas states so eloquently, "As the saints in heaven are free from all need, being inebriated with the plenty of God's house (Psalm 35:10[30])," they have no need of suffrages.

Do the prayers of the Church, the Mass,
and alms profit the departed?

Recall, if you will, our quotation from *Catechism* no. 1032 three questions back. The Church explicitly commends prayers, Masses, and almsgiving on behalf of the dead. In his own affirmative answer to this question, Thomas places special emphasis on the power of the Eucharist, which is chiefly the sacrament of *charity*

---

[30] Verse 9 in the Douay-Rheims translation. The corresponding verse in the RSVCE reads, "They feast on the abundance of your house" (36:8).

because it contains Him who joins the Church together in unity. In that sense, it is the very *origin* and *bond* of charity. Indeed, because the Eucharist provides this supernatural unity born of charity, "its effect can pass to another, which is not the case with the other sacraments." A chief *effect* of charity is *almsgiving*, which can profit all members of the Church who have not already arrived in heaven. These two, then, are the chief suffrages for the dead. As far as *intention* directed to the dead, however, the chief suffrage is prayer, "because prayer by its very nature implies relation not only to the person who prays, even as other works do, but more directly still to that which we pray for." For these reasons, the Holy Sacrifice of the Mass, almsgiving, and prayer are the principal means of aiding the dead, but "any other goods whatsoever that are done out of charity for the dead are profitable to them."

Do the indulgences of the Church profit the dead?

I don't know about you, but I rarely hear indulgences discussed anymore. Thomas cites preaching a crusade and visiting a shrine as examples of actions that earn indulgences, so it seems best to preface Thomas's answer to this question with some background from the *Catechism*, which addresses indulgences in paragraphs 1471–1479 and 1498.

In brief, an indulgence refers to the partial or complete remission of the temporal punishments of venial sins or mortal sins that have already been forgiven, but not yet satisfied through adequate penitential acts. Sins produce a "double consequence": first, mortal sins deprive us of communion with God and render us incapable of attaining eternal life. Further, both mortal sins and venial sins involve an unhealthy attachment to temporal things, which must be purified before we can enter heaven. Purification, here or in purgatory, frees us from those "temporal punishments" that are the second consequence of sins. Closely related to the sacrament of Penance is the Church's power to grant indulgences through the faculty of binding and loosing that Christ bestowed upon her (see Matt. 16:19; 18:18). A *partial* remittance of temporal punishment is referred to as a partial indulgence, while a plenary indulgence obtains complete remission of temporal punishment. Indulgences are made possible by the merits of the saints in heaven, which create a spiritual "treasury" that the Church can share with the faithful on earth and in purgatory, who are united to the saints through charity. We can earn an indulgence by performing extra-sacramental actions or practicing devotions that are promulgated by the Church, but are not *required* of the faithful. Examples include reciting specific prayers, using particular religious objects, and going on pilgrimages.

As for Thomas's answer to our question, indulgences always profit the person who performs them, but when the Church grants an indulgence specifying something to the effect that the person or "'his father, or any other person connected with him and detained in purgatory, will gain so much indulgence,'" an indulgence of this kind will avail not only a living but also a deceased person." We should be well aware, however, that since Thomas's time, the Church has changed how she administers indulgences. Today, "indulgences *can* always *be applied to oneself or to the souls of the deceased*, but they cannot be applied to other persons living on earth."[31] While the Church cannot release

---

[31] Apostolic Penitentiary, "The Gift of the Indulgence," January 29, 2000, no. 7, http://www.vatican.va/roman_curia/tribunals/apost_penit/documents/rc_trib_appen_pro_20000129_indulgence_en.html. Italics original.

souls from purgatory without a lawful cause, when there is a fitting reason for an indulgence, nothing hinders the Church from distributing the common merits of the saints to either the living or the dead.

Do burial services profit the dead?

Burial services are not of *direct* profit to the dead. Thomas rarely uses such terms as "ridiculous" and "absurd," but he does so here when referring to the pagan belief that burial profits the dead because a soul cannot attain rest until the body is buried. Burial provides direct benefits *to the living,* offering consolation through the opportunity to remember and honor the dead. Still, burial does profit the dead *indirectly,* as it motivates the living to pity and pray for the souls of their departed loved ones, and to do other good works on their behalf, such as assisting the poor. Indeed, we see this in our own day when we make contributions to the Church or some particular charity or cause on behalf of the deceased. For these reasons, burying the dead is among the seven corporal works of mercy traditionally specified by the Church.[32]

Do suffrages offered for one deceased person profit others as well?

Perhaps the most interesting argument that suffrages do *not* necessarily profit only the person for whom they are offered builds

---

[32] "The corporal works of mercy consist especially in feeding the hungry, sheltering the homeless, clothing the naked, visiting the sick and imprisoned, and burying the dead" (CCC 2447). Thomas addresses the corporal and spiritual works of mercy in depth in the ten articles of ST, II-II, 32, "Almsdeeds."

upon the words of Christ: "Blessed are you poor, for yours is the kingdom of God" (Luke 6:20). The argument holds that since the poor tend to have fewer suffrages offered for them than the rich, they would be less blessed than the rich if the suffrages for the latter did not also profit them. Thomas replies that there is nothing to stop the rich from being better off than the poor in some respects, in terms of the expiation (atonement) of their punishment, because "this is as nothing in comparison with the kingdom of heaven, where the poor are shown to be better off by the authority quoted."

Thomas explains that human justice reflects divine justice. According to human justice, when a person pays another's debt, he releases that debt alone. So too, according to divine justice, do suffrages pay only the debt of the person for whom they are offered. And yet, since the value of suffrages derives from "the virtue of charity, which makes all goods common," there is a sense in which suffrages may also profit those who are most full of charity, providing not remittance of punishment but a special consolation, because those who possess charity rejoice in the fact that another person experiences good after death in the form of reduced punishment. (What a wonderful, loving side effect of the virtue of charity!)

Are general suffrages offered for several people as valuable as particular suffrages offered for individuals?

Thomas echoes Augustine's claim that joy increases when it is shared by many. This means that many in purgatory will rejoice through *charity* at any good deed performed for a particular soul. Still, according to divine justice, suffrages have "finite efficiency" for the remission of punishment. If a suffrage is divided among many souls, it aids each one less than if were offered for a single person. This is why Church is wise to offer some Masses for one particular person rather than for all the faithful departed.

Do general suffrages suffice to deliver souls
who do not receive special suffrages?

No, they do not. Again, we should also offer special suffrages for particular people. Thomas notes that "although the power of Christ Who is contained in the Sacrament of the Eucharist is infinite, yet there is a definite effect to which that sacrament is directed." In other words, a single Mass offered for the faithful departed in general does *not* fully expiate the punishment of all souls in purgatory. Likewise, one sacrifice does not suffice to release a man completely from the satisfaction due for his sins. This is why several Masses may be offered for the remission of one person's sins — even if the person no longer needs suffrages. We believe that God, through His mercy, will apply those suffrages *to others* who do need them. As St. John Damascene declared in his sermon on those who sleep in the Faith, "'Truly God, forasmuch as He is just will adapt ability to the disabled, and will arrange for an exchange of deficiencies': and this exchange is effected when what is lacking to one is supplied by another."

7

Why We Should Pray to the Saints

God alone of Himself knows the thoughts of the heart: yet others know them, in so far as these are revealed to them, either by their vision of the Word or by any other means.

—ST, Supplement, 72, 1

Do the saints hear our prayers?

Our *Catechism* states clearly that the saints who precede us into heaven serve as "a cloud of witnesses." Further, "they contemplate God, praise him and constantly care for those whom they have left on earth" (2683). In the parable of the talents, Jesus told us that God's faithful servants will be placed in charge over much when they enter into the joy of the Master (Matt. 25:21, 23). The prayers they offer up for us are part of their exalted service, and we should pray to them "to intercede for us and for the whole world" (CCC 2683).

Of course, as we saw in chapter 2, separated souls lack bodily senses (to be restored at the Last Judgment). The saints have no ears, so how do they hear our prayers? Thomas explains that the saints in heaven see the divine essence, which is sufficient for knowing all things necessary. God, by beholding His own essence, knows all there is. No creature, including the saints and the highest angels, can completely comprehend God's essence and thereby know everything, but each of the blessed does see in God's essence "as many other things as the perfection of his happiness requires." Part of the saints' service to God is helping us attain our salvation, "for thus they become God's co-operators, 'than which nothing is more Godlike,' as Dionysius declares." Hence, they know not through senses, but through the Word of God, "the vows, devotions, and prayers of those who have recourse to their assistance."

Thomas also notes that while the saints know the woes and sufferings of their loved ones on earth, this does not produce grief in the saints, because they are so full of heavenly joy that they can know no sorrow whatsoever.

Should we ask the saints to pray for us?

We saw that our *Catechism* tells us we should pray to the saints for our own benefit and for the benefit of others. Elaborating on this truth, Thomas first cites Job 5:1: "Call now, is there any one who will answer you? To which of the holy ones will you turn?" Commenting on this verse, Gregory explained that we call on God in prayer, and the saints are the holy ones to whom we turn so they may pray to God for us. Further, St. Paul requested prayers for himself from the faithful here on earth (Rom. 15:30), whom Thomas called saints "on the way." The saints who have already arrived, so to speak, are closer still to God. Their prayers are more acceptable to Him, so we have even more reason to ask them to help us with their prayers. Moreover, it has long been the Church's custom to ask the saints for their intercession in the Litany of the Saints.[33]

---

[33] An online version of that beautiful prayer can be found at https://www.ewtn.com/catholicism/devotions/litany-of-the-saints-250.

Thomas elaborates with insights from Dionysius, who wrote that God so ordered creation that "the last should be led to God by those that are midway between." The saints in heaven are nearest to God, and divine law requires that we, the "pilgrims" on earth, should be brought to God by the saints who reside between us and Him. Thomas makes clear that although God employs "secondary causes," such the intercessory aid of the saints, to work out His will, this in no way suggests a lack in His power. To the contrary, it illustrates how God so perfectly ordered the universe that He not only pours out His goodness on us, but also provides us with the capacity *to cause goodness* in others.

If you pray to the saints yourself, you may have wondered whether, if some saints are especially holy and close to God, we should pray to any lesser saints. Thomas, of course, has the answer (five answers, to be precise). Though the greater saints are closer to and more acceptable to God than the lesser ones, there are five reasons we should pray to the minor saints too:

1. A person may have a greater devotion to a particular lesser saint, and the effects of prayers are strengthened by the intensity of one's devotion.
2. It can become tedious or boring to pay attention to just one thing. If we occasionally pray to a different saint, the "fervor of our devotion is aroused anew."
3. God has given us particular saints as patrons over particular cases.[34] St. Anthony of Egypt, for example, is invoked "against the fire of hell."
4. We can give the honor due to all the saints.

---

[34] In 1880, Pope Leo XIII declared St. Thomas himself the patron saint of Catholic students and schools.

5. The prayers of several saints may sometimes achieve
what the prayers of only one saint do not.

What wonderful reasons to learn about and pray to a variety of
saints!

Are the prayers of the saints for us always granted?

Thomas begins his answers to six objections by describing the
incident when the prophet Jeremiah, who had been dead for
over four hundred years, appeared to Judah Maccabee and the
high priest Onias in response to the priest's prayers for the Jewish
people (2 Macc. 15:12–16). Jeremiah offered Judas a holy sword
as a gift of God and told him he would use it to strike down his
enemies. This prayer was indeed answered, as the Jews defeated
the Seleucid army the next day. Next, Thomas cites Jerome,
who wrote that if the great apostles and martyrs were able to
pray effectively for others while still in the flesh and "solicitous
for themselves," how much more can they achieve through their
prayers "when the crown, the victory, the triumph is already
theirs!"

Thomas explains that the prayers of the saints for us *are always
granted.* This is because the saints in heaven will only what God
wills, and what God wills is always fulfilled. We must consider
two qualifications, however.

First, earlier in the *Summa* (I, 19, 6), Thomas thoroughly
discusses the fulfillment of God's will. God's simple or absolute
will that a particular thing happen is always fulfilled. What God
decrees *must* happen *does.* Still, we can speak of God's antecedent will, which Thomas says "may be called a willingness rather
than an absolute will." (Some in the Church today speak of God's
"permissive" will, as contrasted with His "active" or "positive"

will.) Further, according to Thomas, "whatever God simply wills takes place; although what He wills antecedently may not take place." This is because God has given humans and angels the freedom to make choices according to their own wills, which may, through sin, choose things contrary to God's will.

Thomas provides an earthly example of a just judge who wills all men to live (*antecedent* will), but who *consequently* and rightly condemns a man to be hanged because he is "a murderer or dangerous to society." In the same sense, "God antecedently wills all men to be saved, but consequently wills some to be damned, as His justice exacts." This, too, applies to the saints: they pray *antecedently* that all men be saved, but only according to God's divine justice, which has given men their own free will.

As for a second qualification, Thomas addresses the objection that since the saints pray only for what they know is in accord with God's will, we shouldn't bother praying to them at all, since what God directly wills would be accomplished even without their prayers. Thomas replies that the prayers of the saints can still be efficacious in cases where *God has preordained* that people will be saved *through* the intercession of those saints. (The same, of course, applies to us here on earth. God wills that we pray to Him for what we need, and Christ Himself has instructed us to pray "Thy will be done.")

8

Last Thoughts on the Last Things: Death

*Let us begin with the remembrance of the first of these four last
things, which is undoubtedly, by far, the least of the four. From
that one we shall make a proof of what a marvelous effect can
come of the diligent remembrance of all four toward the avoiding
of all the snares, darts, tricks, enticing, and assaults of the three
mortal enemies: the devil, the world, and our own flesh.*

—St. Thomas More, *The Four Last Things*[35]

As we come to some last thoughts on death, the first of the
Last Things, we might recall some highlights of the whirlwind
Thomistic tour we took in our first seven chapters. We saw how
after the death and corruption of our bodies, and before the resurrection, our immaterial, spiritual souls will continue to exist
in their proper place. The destination of our souls is determined
by whether we die in God's grace, and the journey to our resting place depends on the nature and extent of any lingering,
unsatisfied punishment for forgiven mortal sins and the guilt or
punishment for venial sins. We examined the reality and nature

---

[35] Thomas More, *The Four Last Things, The Supplication of Souls,
A Dialogue on Conscience* (New York: Scepter, 2002), 22.

of purgatory, limbo, and "Abraham's bosom." We examined lessons from Thomas, the Church Fathers, and the Magisterium of the Catholic Church on issues we can be certain of, as well as mysteries that we can understand only in heaven. We saw the need to pray, offer Masses, and do pious works for the sake of the Church Suffering, to which our brothers and sisters in purgatory belong. We saw how God has raised the saints to heaven and enabled the members of the Church Triumphant to help us get there too. We examined many fascinating and beautiful ways that God's divine justice, mercy, and charity operate not only in life but also eternally, even after death.

Of course, our tour of the spiritual realities that immediately follow death, as profound and awe-inspiring as they are, was not undertaken merely out of curiosity or even for sublime intellectual stimulation. These mysterious realities describe the eternity that awaits us at the end of our brief earthly lives. *They should determine how we live every day of our lives here on earth.*

St. Thomas More (1478–1535) points out that though it is "by far the least" of the Four Last Things, contemplating the reality of our death can produce a "marvelous" effect upon us in life. He notes that of the Four Last Things, only death looms inevitable for all people, even those without faith. Indeed, More states that the most profound of the ancient pagan philosophers considered philosophy—the love (*philos*) of wisdom (*sophia*)—as a proper preparation or practice for the inevitability of death. They believed that as death separates the soul from the body, the study of philosophy, by bringing the passions under reason's control, frees the soul from the dictates of the body's loves and affections while the two are still united. According to More, nothing more effectively severs our souls from the passions of our bodies than the thought of death, particularly our own death. We should not contemplate the reality of our death casually, but *allow it to sink deep into our hearts through intense imagination.*

Chances are you and I do indeed think seriously about death at times, at least following the death and funeral of a loved one. If we are truly wise, we will contemplate our own inevitable death as well. How often do you stop to think that one day *you* will be that person whose body is lowered back down into the earth from whence you came?[36] Life as we now know it will be gone, as will our last chance to cooperate with God's grace so that we may spend eternity with Him. Thinking about our own death will help us to remain close to God and withstand the snares and enticements of the devil, the world, and the flesh. The world and the flesh will no longer be ours, and we certainly don't want our souls to belong to the devil.

Our *Catechism* makes clear that we should all remember our mortality, as it "helps us realize that we have only a limited time in which to bring our lives to fulfillment" (1007). Further, the *Catechism* encourages us to "prepare ourselves for the hour of our death" (1014). Indeed, when we pray the Hail Mary, asking the Blessed Mother of God to "pray for us sinners, now and at the hour of our death," we would do well to let our thoughts linger on the reality of that last hour, which will likely take us all by surprise.

---

[36] I review these words on March 23, 2020. I first wrote them a few months ago, shortly before the coronavirus pandemic, which most likely has more people around the world seriously pondering their own mortality than any other time in recent memory.

Part 2

Judgment Day

Now at His first coming when Christ came to be judged, He appeared in the form of weakness. Therefore at the second coming, when He will come to judge, He will appear in the form of glory.

—ST, Supplement, 90, 2

9

Signs That Will Precede the Last Judgment

When Christ shall come to judge He will appear in the
form of glory, on account of the authority becoming a
judge. Now it pertains to the dignity of judicial power to
have certain signs that induce people to reverence and
subjection: and consequently many signs will precede the
advent of Christ when He shall come to judgment.

—ST, Supplement, 73, 1

Will there be signs before the Last Judgment?

As we see in our opening quotation, the answer is yes. It would
seem to be an open-and-shut case, since "it is written (Luke
21:25): 'There shall be signs in the sun, and in the moon, and
in the stars,' etc." Yet 1 Thessalonians 5:2–3 notes, seemingly to
the contrary, that the Lord will come "like a thief in the night"
when people proclaim there is "peace and security." In response,
Thomas draws on Augustine's insight that those who proclaim
peace and security are the wicked, who will pay no attention to
the signs of the impending Last Judgment.

Thomas also cites Jerome, who, elaborating on passages from
Scripture (such as Matt. 24:29 and Luke 21:25), listed a full *fifteen*

signs, including changes in the sun, stars, mountains, animals, and so on. These signs will culminate on the Last Day, when "all will die and rise again with those who died long before." The Lord is said to come "like a thief in the night" because, despite the signs, it will still not be possible to know the *exact time* of the Last Judgment.

Will the sun and moon grow dark near the Last Judgment?

This interesting question builds upon Matthew 24:29, which mentions that "the sun will be darkened, and the moon will not give its light" after the time of the final tribulation, just before the return of Christ.[37] Rabanus (780–856), a Benedictine monk and theologian, argued that the sun, moon, and stars could well lose their light at the same time, as the sun did at the time of Christ's Passion.

Thomas begins his reply to this and two other arguments that the heavenly bodies will become dark with an interesting appeal not to Scripture or the Fathers, but to the science of astronomy! Astronomers tell us that the sun and the moon cannot be eclipsed at the same time, so if both were darkened simultaneously, it could not be due to a *natural* eclipse. Further, Thomas recalls the words of Isaiah 30:26, which declare that "the light of the moon will be as the light of the sun, and the light of the sun will be sevenfold."

Thomas concludes that *after* Christ comes, the saints and the whole world will be renewed, and there will be not perpetual

---

[37] While explicating the line "From thence He will come again to judge the living and the dead" from the Apostles' Creed, CCC 675–677 addresses "the Church's ultimate trial."

darkness, but an *increase* in light. Still, immediately *before* the Last Judgment, God could indeed use *His divine power* to darken the sun and the heavenly bodies, at various times or all at once, "in order to inspire men with fear."

Will the angels in heaven be moved when our Lord arrives?

Some have argued that angels could not be said to be moved at the Last Judgment. According to Aristotle, ignorance is the cause of wonder. Gregory adds that angels see all through seeing God, so there is no ignorance in them. Further, we see in Revelation 7:11 that the angels will stand around God's throne at the Last Judgment; therefore, they will not be moved.

Thomas answers by referencing Job 26:11: "The pillars of heaven tremble, and are astounded at his rebuke." He also cites Matthew 24:29, which states that "the powers of the heavens will be shaken." In the Latin Bible Thomas used, the word translated above as "powers" was *virtutes*, or "virtues." Building on the insights of Gregory, Thomas explains that the word "virtues" can be applied to a *particular order* of angels, the fifth of nine orders in the angelic hierarchy,[38] but it can also refer to angels *in general*. Though angels are not culpably ignorant of anything, they do not, like God, know all there is to know. Since wonder concerns things that surpass one's knowledge or abilities, the angels in heaven will indeed be moved by wonder at the Last Judgment, as God by His divine power does things even they cannot fully comprehend. What a remarkable thing for us to ponder — and look forward to!

---

[38] See *ST*, I, 108 for Thomas's description of the angelic hierarchy.

10

On the Fire of the Final Conflagration

Since the world was, in a way, made for man's sake,
it follows that, when man shall be glorified in the body,
the other bodies of the world shall also be changed
to a better state, so that it is rendered a more fitting
place for him and more pleasant to look upon.

—*ST*, Supplement, 74, 1

Will the world be cleansed at the Last Judgment?

Some people argue that the world will not be cleansed at the
Last Judgment. Regarding animals, reptiles, and birds, Acts 10:15
states, "What God has cleansed, you must not call common."
Accordingly, the things of creation are not unclean and will not
need cleansing.

Thomas replies, however, that all renewal is made possible by
some kind of cleansing. Furthermore, Scripture tells us, "Then I
saw a new heaven and new earth; for the first heaven and the first
earth had passed away, and the sea was no more" (Rev. 21:1). Not
only man but also the world itself will be glorified, and in order
to glorify something, "it behooves first of all those things to be
removed which are opposed to glory. There are two, namely the

corruption and stain of sin—because according to 1 Corinthians 15:50, 'neither shall corruption possess incorruption,' and all the unclean shall be without the city of glory (Apocalypse 22:15)." While physical elements cannot sin, they can be made unfit for receiving the perfection of glory if sins are committed in them, much as a crime scene would be unfit for sacred purposes unless it is first cleaned. Contrary to the Manicheans, who said that evil, like good, is in the substance of things, Thomas clarifies that *all creatures of God are good in themselves.* They are not unclean in their nature or their substance, *but they do acquire accidental imperfections that will be cleansed at the end of the world.*

Will the world be cleansed by fire?

Some argue from reason that fire cannot produce the cleansing of the world, because fire itself is a part of the world and therefore needs to be cleansed. Others, citing the great flood in the Old Testament, argue that some things need to be cleansed not by fire, but by water.

Thomas replies to the contrary that Scripture clearly states: "Our God comes, he does not keep silence, before him is a devouring fire, round about him a mighty tempest. He calls to the heaven above and to the earth, that he may judge his people" (Ps. 50 [49]:3–4). Further, "[because of] the coming of the day of God ... the heavens will be kindled and dissolved, and the elements will melt with fire!" (2 Pet. 3:12).

Fire will cleanse the world because it is the noblest element and, through its light, most closely resembles glory itself. It is also the element least likely to be contaminated by foreign matter. Fire in its pure state will be the cleansing agent, and to the extent that it is contaminated by foreign matter, this matter will be rarefied and burned away, so that fire "will be cleanser and cleansed under different aspects." As for the cleansing powers of water, the great deluge cleansed the world from the stain of sin and cooled the heat of concupiscence. At the end of the world, the primary sin will be tepidity or lack of spiritual heat, because according to Matthew 24:12, "most men's love will grow cold." Therefore, "the cleansing will then be fittingly effected by fire."[39]

Will the cleansing fire be the same as natural fire?

We read in 2 Peter 3:12 that "the elements will melt with fire," and fire, along with earth, air, and water, is one of the four elements. But since nothing can consume itself, some suppose that the cleansing fire will not be the same as elemental (natural) fire.

However, in a gloss on 1 Corinthians 7:31, Augustine writes that "the fashion of this world will perish in the burning of worldly flames." Further, 2 Peter 3:5–7 compares the great flood in the Old Testament to the fire that will cleanse the world. Thomas comments: "Now in the first cleansing the water was of the same species with elemental water. Therefore in like manner the fire of the second cleansing will be of the same species with elemental fire." Thomas also notes that the cleansing fire, "although the same species as ours, is not identically the same." The cleansing fire produced by God's divine power will possess greater power than elemental fire. Now "the greater destroys the

---

[39] How interesting that centuries before Christ, early pagan Stoic philosophers also taught that the world would end in a great fire. Further, modern astronomers predict that as the sun expands into a red giant, somewhere around five to seven billion years from now, Earth will be consumed within its fires.

lesser by consuming its matter. In like manner that fire [the fire of the final conflagration] will be able to destroy our fire."

Will the fire cleanse the higher heavens?

Some suppose that the fire will cleanse the higher heavens (that is, the celestial sphere) themselves. Psalm 102 [101]:25–26, which declares that the heavens will perish, seems to support this claim. Like Augustine, however, Thomas holds that the fire will cleanse only the "aerial heavens" (that is, the sky), and not the higher celestial realm. As evidence, he cites 2 Peter 3:5–7, which makes clear that the water of the great flood was limited to the aerial heavens. Thomas notes that because the higher heavens have no imperfections, they need no cleansing; rather, at the end of the world, the heavenly bodies will be "set at rest by God's will alone."

Will the fire consume the other elements?

In answering this perhaps rather esoteric question, Thomas makes clear that there are many opinions on the matter. He rejects Bede's claim that two of the elements will be completely destroyed and two will be restored in a better fashion. He also disagrees with what appears to be Augustine's opinion that in the final conflagration, "the qualities of the corruptible elements … will entirely perish by fire: and the substance itself will have those qualities that become an immortal body." Instead, Thomas concludes that the elements will most likely "remain as to their substance and proper qualities," but they will be cleansed from whatever stains and impurities they have contracted through the sins of mankind. Additionally, Thomas clarifies Augustine's position, noting that "this is what Augustine calls the 'qualities of corruptible elements,' namely their unnatural dispositions by reason of which they come near to corruption." In other words, the elements themselves will not be destroyed, but perfected and freed from their "unnatural dispositions."

Will all the elements be cleansed by fire?

Some argue, building on 2 Peter 3:7, that not all the elements will be cleansed, because the fire at the end of the world will not reach higher than the waters of the great flood did. Augustine also wrote that "the same world which perished in the deluge is reserved unto fire," and Thomas notes that the waters of the flood extended only about fifteen feet above the highest mountaintops. Thomas concludes that all the elements "chiefly round about the earth as far as the middle of the air," which were susceptible to corruption by man's sins, will be cleansed by fire, but higher realms will not be cleansed. Heaven will not be cleansed, since it holds no imperfections. Neither will hell be cleansed, since "the dregs of the whole earth will be brought thither," according to Psalm 75 [74]:9, which states that "all the wicked of the earth shall drain it down to the dregs."

Will the fire of the final conflagration occur after the judgment?

All four of the arguments that the final conflagration will come *before* the final judgment seem interesting, plausible, and authoritative. Here they are, in brief:

1. Augustine gave the following order of events at the Last Judgment: "Elias the Thesbite [Elijah] will appear, the Jews will believe, [the] Antichrist will persecute,

Christ will judge, the dead shall rise again, the good shall be separated from the wicked, the world shall be set on fire and shall be renewed." Therefore, the burning comes after the judgment.

2. Augustine also said, "After the wicked have been judged, and cast into everlasting fire, the figure of this world will perish in the furnace of worldly flames."

3. Further, we read in 1 Thessalonians 4:16–17 that when the Lord returns to judge, He will find people still alive.

4. Finally, our Lord is said to come again to judge the earth by fire, so it would seem that the final conflagration is the execution of the sentence of divine judgment. "Now execution follows judgment. Therefore this fire will follow the judgment."

Thomas begins his response with the clear words of Psalm 97 [96]:3: "Fire goes before him." Then, he argues that the resurrection will come before the judgment so that all people can see Christ judge the world. Further, the fire will come before the resurrection, because the saints who are raised will have "spiritual and impassible bodies, so that it will be impossible for the fire to cleanse them,[40] and yet the text [of Lombard's *Sentences*] ... quotes Augustine ... as saying that 'whatever needs cleansing in any way shall be cleansed by that fire.' Therefore that fire will precede the judgment."

Thomas concludes that the final fire, "so far as it shall cleanse the world, will precede the judgment, but as regards a certain action thereof, whereby it will engulf the wicked, it will follow

---

[40] In chapter 18, we will examine the nature of these spiritual, impassible, glorified bodies.

the judgment." He replies as follows to the objections mentioned earlier:

1. Augustine himself makes clear that the order he presents is just his opinion and a matter of faith, adding that "how and in what order we shall learn more then by experience of the things themselves than now by seeking a definite conclusion by arguing about them."
2. The above applies as well to Augustine's second comment on the order of events.
3. According to Thomas, "all men shall die and rise again: yet those are said to be found alive who will live in the body until the time of the conflagration."
4. The fire will execute the sentence of the judge only as it regards the engulfing of the damned. *In this respect,* the fire will follow the judgment.

What effects will the fire have on men?

Thomas explains that the fire occurring *before* the Last Judgment will act as an instrument of divine justice and will reduce to ashes the bodies of both the good and the wicked still living at the time. The wicked will be tortured by the fire, but

> the good in whom there will be nothing to cleanse will feel no pain at all from the fire, as neither did the children in the fiery furnace (Daniel 3); although their bodies will not be kept whole, as were the bodies of the children: and it will be possible by God's power for their bodies to be destroyed without their suffering pain. But the good, in whom matter for cleansing will be found, will suffer pain from that fire, more or less according to their different merits.

Still, *after* the judgment, the fire will act only on the damned, "since the good will all have impassible bodies."

Will the fire engulf the wicked?

Thomas says the final conflagration will cleanse and renew mankind. One way man will be cleansed is the separation of the wicked from the good, as Luke 3:17 says: "His winnowing fork is in his hand, to clear his threshing floor, and to gather the wheat into his granary, but the chaff he will burn with unquenchable fire." So too, at the final conflagration, all that is ugly and vile will be cast with the wicked into hell, while everything beautiful and noble will be taken up to heaven for the glory of those who are saved. St. Basil of Caesarea (A.D. 330–379) made this point in a gloss on Psalm 29 [28]:7 ("The voice of the Lord flashes forth flames of fire"). Whatever gross matter is contained in the fire will be thrust into hell for the punishment of the wicked, and "whatever is subtle and lightsome will remain above for the glory of the elect," says Thomas.

11

Of the Resurrection

*The gift of Christ is greater than the sin of Adam, as appears
from Romans 5:15. Now death was brought in by sin, for
if sin had not been, there had been no death. Therefore by
the gift of Christ man will be restored from death to life.*

—ST, Supplement, 75, 1

Will our bodies be resurrected?

The first of five objections to the resurrection of the body comes
from Job 14:12: "So man lies down and rises not again; till the
heavens are no more he will not awake, or be roused out of his
sleep." There will not come a time when the heavens are no more,
since even the earth "remains for ever" (Eccles. 1:4). Therefore,
the dead will never rise again.

Thomas begins his response with another passage from the
book of Job: "For I know that my Redeemer lives, and at last
he will stand upon the earth; and after my skin has been thus
destroyed, then from my flesh I shall see God" (19:25–26). Therefore, Thomas says, there will be a resurrection of the body. Next,
he elaborates on the resurrection as the great free gift from Christ
(Rom. 5:15), as we see in this chapter's opening quotation.

Thomas cites Augustine to explain that some philosophers, such as the Neoplatonist Porphyrius (A.D. 233–305), denied the resurrection because of their false belief that bodily things originate from an evil principle, while spiritual things come from a good principle. Therefore, they argued, the soul can reach perfection only when it casts off the body. Others, including Plato himself, said that man's entire nature is seated in the soul and the body is merely its instrument, as a ship is to a sailor. Full happiness, they maintained, can be obtained through things of the soul alone, so there is no need for a bodily resurrection. Quite interestingly, Thomas cites Aristotle's book *On the Soul*, noting that "the Philosopher sufficiently destroys this foundation … where he shows that the soul is united to the body as form to matter.[41] Hence it is clear that if man cannot be happy in this life, we must of necessity hold the resurrection."

Thomas says that since our good works on earth are performed by the composite of body and soul, it is fitting that both body and soul receive the rewards for these works. As for the verse in Job (14:12) that states the heavens will never be broken, this refers to their substance, but not to the specific effects of their power by which their movement causes the generation and corruption of lower things. Such movements and effects will not remain after the heavens are renewed and things no longer degenerate or undergo corruption. This is what "the Apostle" (St. Paul) means when he writes, "The form of this world is passing away" (1 Cor. 7:31).

---

[41] Cf. CCC 365: "The unity of soul and body is so profound that one has to consider the soul to be the 'form' of the body: i.e., it is because of its spiritual soul that the body made of matter becomes a living, human body; spirit and matter, in man, are not two natures united, but rather their union forms a single nature."

Will absolutely every person be resurrected?

Two of five objections to the idea that everyone will be resurrected cite what seem to be rather clear pronouncements from the Old Testament: "The wicked will not stand in the judgment" (Ps.1:5) and "Many of those who sleep in the dust of the earth shall awake" (Dan. 12:2). Thomas replies to the contrary with two straightforward passages from the New Testament: "All who are in the tombs will hear his voice and come forth ... and those who hear will live" (John 5:28–29, 25) and "We shall not all sleep, but we shall all be changed" (1 Cor. 15:51).

Thomas elaborates that all humans are members of the same species. Every one of us is a composite of body and soul and cannot attain perfection while the body and soul remain separate. Therefore, all of us must rise again. The verse from Psalm 1 mentioning that the wicked will not rise again refers either to the fact that their bodies will not rise at the time of the particular judgment, or to the wicked who are complete unbelievers, as noted in John 3:18: "He who does not believe is condemned already." The "many" referred to in Daniel 12:2 may actually be "all," for Augustine notes that this signification is often found in the language of Holy Scripture. Or the verse may refer to the children of limbo, who, though they will arise again, could be said not to awaken completely "since they will have no sense either of pain or of glory, and waking is the unchaining of the senses."[42]

---

[42] This "unchaining of the senses" should call to mind the state of the soul and its inability to experience sensation while separated from the body, which Thomas addressed in *ST*, Supplement, 70 (covered in chapter 2).

Is the resurrection natural?

If you'll forgive me the colloquialism, one could certainly say in regard to bodily resurrection, "Now there's something you don't see every day!" We certainly do not see the dead arise very often, and the cases we know of were caused by divine miracles. Interestingly enough, however, Thomas provides five objections that the resurrection is, in a sense, a natural phenomenon. Gregory, for example, wrote that reason provides several examples of natural resurrection, such as the following: light is removed from our sight each night and returns each morning; plants lose their greenery and, by a kind of resurrection, regrow it; and a seed dies and rots, but then sprouts again to new life (as "the Apostle" tells us in 1 Corinthians 15:36: "What you sow does not come to life unless it dies"). Further, unnatural things do not tend to last long, but the resurrected life will last forever.

Thomas responds to the contrary: "There is no natural return from privation to habit.[43] But death is privation of life. Therefore the resurrection whereby one returns from death to life is not natural." Further, by nature, humans are always begotten by human parents, and this will not be the case at the resurrection. Thomas explains that the resurrection is natural only in the very restricted sense that the body always retains a "passive potentiality" for union with the soul, but their reunion after separation exceeds the power of nature and requires a supernatural, miraculous action. The examples provided by Gregory and Paul are useful not in showing us that the resurrection is natural, but by illustrating how through observation of natural things, we can

---

[43] This might call to mind the Scholastic philosophical principle that "a thing cannot give what it does not have."

reason inductively[44] about things that are *above* nature, "since the natural bears a certain resemblance to the supernatural." Another sublime example of this resemblance, per "the Master," Peter Lombard, is how the union of the body and soul resembles "the union of the soul with God by the glory of fruition."

---

[44] That is, from specific observations to general principles.

12

The Cause of Our Resurrection

*In Christ has our resurrection begun, and His resurrection
is the cause of ours. Thus Christ as God is, as it were,
the equivocal cause of our resurrection, but as God
and man rising again, He is the proximate and, so
to say, the univocal cause of our resurrection.*

—*ST*, Supplement, 76, 1

Is Christ's Resurrection the cause of our own?

Some believe that Christ's Resurrection is not the cause of our
own because effects follow their causes, and when Christ arose,
others did not rise with Him. Others note that effects bear a
likeness to their causes, but the resurrection of the wicked will
have no resemblance to the Resurrection of Christ.

Thomas starts his response with some rather heady meta-
physics from Aristotle: "In every genus that which is first is the
cause of those that come after it." Thomas says that because of
His Resurrection, Christ is called "the first fruits of those that
have fallen asleep" (1 Cor. 15:20) and "the first-born of the dead"
(Rev. 1:5). "Therefore," Thomas concludes, "His resurrection is
the cause of the resurrection of others."

Thomas elaborates that Christ, because of His nature as God and man, is called the mediator of God and men; consequently, "the Divine gifts are bestowed on men by means of Christ's humanity." Just as we are freed from *spiritual* death by God's grace, we are freed from *bodily* death through Christ's Resurrection, brought about by divine power. Christ's grace causes our grace, as St. John says: "From his fulness have we all received, grace upon grace" (John 1:16).

Thomas then clarifies the manner of causation with the quotation that starts this chapter. Christ, in that He is *God*, is the *equivocal cause* of our resurrection (an equivocal cause being a cause that is nobler or of higher order than its effects), while Christ, in that He is *man*, is the *proximate cause* (secondary, lower order, and more immediate) and the *univocal cause* (a cause of the same type as its effect, as when fire causes fire) as well. In sum, the cause of our resurrection is the same as the cause of Christ's, "namely the power of Christ's Godhead which is common to Him and the Father. Hence it is written (Romans 8:11): 'He that raised up Jesus Christ from the dead shall quicken also your mortal bodies.'"

As for the first objection we highlighted, a cause need not produce its full effect immediately, as we can see from the gradual effects of applying heat to an object (think of placing a log in a fire). God willed that our resurrection, caused by Christ's, will happen at the time He has decided. As for the other objection,[45] on the dissimilarity between the resurrection of the wicked and that of Christ, there will still be a natural similarity even for the wicked, in that they were conformed to Christ in their human nature and will rise again to eternal life, "but in the saints who

---

[45] Objection 4 in *ST*, Supplement, 76, 1.

were conformed to Christ by grace, there will be conformity as to things pertaining to glory."

Will the blast of a trumpet cause our resurrection?

This intriguing question arises from differing interpretations of 1 Thessalonians 4:16: "For the Lord himself will descend from heaven ... with the sound of the trumpet of God. And the dead in Christ will rise." Some argue that it would be useless to sound a trumpet to rouse the dead, since they cannot hear; others claim that even if God, through a miracle, gave the sound of the trumpet the power to cause the resurrection, the moment the trumpet had that power, it would act naturally, as when a man born blind whose sight is restored by a miracle then sees naturally. This would imply that the cause of the resurrection is natural, which, as we have seen, is false.

Thomas begins by citing 1 Thessalonians 4:16, as noted above. He elaborates that the dead in their graves will hear the voice of the Son of God and live (John 5:25, 28), and that according to Lombard, "this voice is called the trumpet." Christ's rising as a man is the univocal cause of our resurrection, and it is fitting that Christ would commence the resurrection by "the giving of some common bodily sign." Some say this will be Christ's voice, as when He commanded the sea to be calmed (Matt. 8:26). Others say the sign will be *visibly* manifest: "For as the lightning comes from the east and shines as far as the west, so will be the coming of the Son of man" (Matt. 24:27). Gregory stated that Christ's visible presence is called His voice because as soon as He appears, nature will obey His command to restore human bodies. "Hence He is described as coming 'with commandment' (1 Thessalonians 4:15)." Thomas also notes that in the Old Testament, "by the trumpet they were summoned to the council, stirred to the battle, and called to the feast; and those who rise again will be summoned to the council of judgment, to the battle in which 'the world shall fight ... against the unwise (Wisdom 5:21), and to the feast of everlasting solemnity."

Thomas answers the objection about the dead's lack of hearing with a fascinating comparison to the power of the sacraments, which sanctify "not through being heard, but through being spoken." The voice or trumpet of Christ will not need to be heard by human ears to produce its effect. This same principle answers the other objection. The trumpet or voice of Christ will not operate through natural power, but through the kind of divine power that operates through the sacraments.

Will the angels play a role in our resurrection?

According to 1 Thessalonians 4:16, "the Lord himself will descend from heaven with a cry of command, with the archangel's call." Still, some argue that the angels will probably not be involved in the resurrection, because they play no role when a person's soul is first infused into the body, and the raising of the dead requires a greater power than begetting human beings does. Others argue that if the angels are involved, raising the dead would be a fitting task for the order known as the "virtues," which exercise miraculous powers, and yet Scripture refers to an archangel.[46]

---

[46] Drawing on Scripture, Gregory, and Dionysius, Thomas lists the orders of angels, from highest to lowest, as seraphim, cherubim, thrones, dominations, virtues, powers, principalities, archangels, and angels. He describes their characteristics and roles in *ST*, I, 108.

Thomas answers that 1 Thessalonians 4:16 makes clear that the angels will indeed be involved in the resurrection. Further, Augustine writes that lesser bodily creatures are ruled in a sense by higher bodily creatures, and all bodily creatures are "ruled by God by the rational spirit of life." Gregory described the same idea in his *Dialogues*. Thomas concludes that God uses the ministry of angels in all His works pertaining to bodies. In the case of the resurrection, the angels will gather together all the human *bodily* remains that are to be restored, while the *soul*, as it is immediately created by God Himself, will be reunited with the body by God alone. Further, God Himself will glorify the body without the assistance of angels, just as He glorifies man's soul. Lombard explained that the bodily ministry of the angels is called their "voice" or "call" in 1 Thessalonians 4:16.

As for the seemingly fitting role for the angels known as virtues, Thomas says that the archangel referred to in Scripture is Michael, "who is the prince of the Church as he was of the Synagogue (Daniel 10:13–21)." Still, Michael will act under the influence of the virtues and the higher orders, "so that what he shall do, the higher orders will, in a way, do also." Further, Thomas provides the beautiful insight that the lower angels will help as well; indeed, each of us will be assisted by his own guardian angel. So the "voice" or "call" "can be ascribed either to one or to many angels."

13

When and How All Will Arise

*That which is unknown to the angels will be much more
unknown to men; because those things to which men attain
by natural reason are much more clearly and certainly
known to the angels by their natural knowledge.*

—*ST*, Supplement, 77, 2

*Should the resurrection be delayed
until the end of the world?*

Some argue that the resurrection should not be deferred until the end of the world, because Christ, whose Resurrection caused ours, did not wait to arise. Further, Christ, the Head of the Church, is the cause of the resurrection of her members. As Jerome indicated, according to pious tradition, certain of the most noble members closest to the Head, such as the Blessed Virgin and John the Evangelist, are believed to have been assumed into heaven before the end of the world. Therefore, other noble people closest to the Head should be resurrected before the end of the world. Indeed, even some Old Testament Fathers rose again when Christ rose, per Matthew 27:52: "Many bodies of the saints who had fallen asleep were raised." The other Old

Testament saints, then, should not have to wait until the end of the world. Finally, time will cease after the end of the world, and yet Revelation 20:4–5 tells of martyrs who came to life and reigned with Christ for one thousand years, while "the rest of the dead did not come to life until the thousand years were ended."

Thomas responds with Job 14:12, which states that people who have fallen asleep will not awaken or rise from sleep "till the heavens are no more." The heavens will cease their movement only at the end of the world, so the resurrection will not occur until then.

As for the first objection, Thomas replies that Christ, the Head, has a unique causality regarding our resurrection, such that the resurrection of any of the members does not cause the resurrection of others. We also saw in our last chapter that causes need not produce their effects immediately. Thomas applies this logic to the second objection. Though some members are closer to the Head and rank higher than others, this does not make them like the Head in possessing the power to be the cause of others. Neither do they have the power to rise before others, since Christ is the exemplar of our resurrection, and they are not. That some have been resurrected prior to the general resurrection evidences a special privilege of God's grace, and is not "due on account of conformity to Christ."

In response to the third objection, Thomas cites a work attributed to Jerome that is now considered spurious. Still, Thomas concludes that it was fitting that some Old Testament Fathers rose to bear witness to Christ's Resurrection. He does clarify that "although the Gospel mentions their resurrection before Christ's, we must take this statement as made in anticipation, as is often the case with writers of history." Nobody rose again in true resurrection before Christ, "since He is the 'first-fruits of them that sleep' (1 Corinthians 15:20), although some were resuscitated before Christ's resurrection, as in the case of Lazarus." Either the Old Testament Fathers were merely resuscitated, or they were raised to witness the Resurrection and then ascended, body and soul, into heaven. The latter, says Thomas, is more probable.

It is important to consider Thomas's response to the final objection. Even in the third and fourth centuries after Christ, there were heretics known as "chiliasts" or "millennialists," who believed that there would be a first resurrection, followed by the earthly reign of the resurrected for one thousand years before the end of the world.[47] Augustine counters that the "first resurrection" mentioned in Scripture is the spiritual resurrection whereby we rise again from sin through the gift of God's grace, while the "second resurrection" is that of the body at the end of the world. The "first resurrection" has already taken place, and Christ already reigns in glory with the martyrs and other saints. The number one thousand is not to be taken literally, but denotes a great, unspecified number, as we see in Psalm 105 [104]:8: "He is mindful of his covenant for ever, of the word that he commanded, for a thousand generations."[48]

---

[47] In our time, religious groups such as Mormons and Jehovah's Witnesses still hold some form of this belief.

[48] An interesting example of the use of figurative numbers in Revelation is found in the *Confession* of St. Patrick. Near the end of his years of slavery in Ireland, a voice told him a ship was ready to take him home, but it was two hundred miles away. As a runaway slave, Patrick, along with anyone who helped him, could have faced death if captured. Nonetheless, Patrick tells us that with God directing his path, he made the journey without fear, and he did indeed gain passage on a ship that returned him to his home and his freedom. For centuries, scholars consulted maps of ancient Ireland, trying to

Is the time of our resurrection hidden?

This seems to be a timeless question. Even in our own time, people have declared, based on the most tenuous of supposedly scientific data, that the world will end as we know it within twelve years or so. Others, based on spurious private interpretations of Scripture, or even ancient Mesoamerican writings, have prepared themselves and their followers for the end of the world on specific calendar dates, only to revise their predictions when the world ignored its expiration date and kept going about its business.

In and before Thomas's time, some people argued, based on particular scriptural texts, that we can deduce the time of the resurrection and the end of the world. They cited, for example, Revelation 12:6, which mentions a period of "one thousand two hundred and sixty days" during which a woman (representing the Church) would be fed. The days actually represent years, they reasoned, as in Ezekiel 4:6: "Forty days I assign you, a day for each year." Further, some argued that the Old Testament foreshadows and prefigures the New Testament, and since we can determine

---

deduce from his mention of two hundred miles exactly where Patrick had been held and where he met the boat that took him home. Thomas O'Loughlin, a modern biographer of St. Patrick, notes that a distance of two hundred miles is equal to the "one thousand six hundred stadia" referred to in Revelation 14:20. The number is used in Scripture to represent a great distance. Patrick, then, may not have been attempting to give any kind of exact measurement of the actual distance. Rather, by the time Patrick wrote his life story, decades after his escape, he had become so immersed in Christian teachings that he practically thought, wrote, and lived in and through the words of Holy Scripture!

exactly when the events of the Old Testament began and ended, we can do the same with the New, since it will last to the end of the world, as stated in Matthew 28:20: "I am with you always, to the close of the age."

Thomas begins his response with this chapter's opening quotation. The knowledge of angels is clearer and more certain than that of humans. Since "not even the angels of heaven" know the time of the resurrection (Matt. 24:36), it makes sense that we cannot know it either. Further, while the apostles had more knowledge of God's secrets than other people, the resurrected Christ said even to them, when they asked for the time of the restoration of the kingdom of Israel, "It is not for you to know times or seasons which the Father has fixed by his own authority" (Acts 1:7).

Thomas cites Augustine's explanation that just as we cannot know how long our old age will last, so too we cannot say with certainty how long our world will continue. The reason for this "is because the exact length of future time cannot be known except either by revelation or by natural reason." Natural reason cannot deduce the time of the resurrection, and it has not yet been revealed. Elaborating on Christ's words to the apostles, Augustine eloquently states a precept that all modern doomsday prophets should heed: "He scatters the fingers of all calculators and bids them be still." Some of Augustine's contemporaries said that Christ would return four hundred years after His Ascension. Others suggested five hundred years; still others, one thousand. Thomas, living more than twelve hundred years after the Ascension, would conclude, "The falseness of these calculators is evident, as will likewise be the falseness of those who even now cease not to calculate." Almost eight hundred years after Thomas's time, heedless of Thomistic wisdom and Church teaching,[49] some false prophets continue to calculate — and re-calculate — while the world keeps on ticking!

Will the resurrection take place at night?

Some believe the resurrection will not take place at night. They point to Job 14:12, which notes the heavens will be no more, and Revelation 10:6, which notes that time will be no more.[50] Both verses suggest there will be no more day or night at the time of the resurrection. Further, we read in 1 Corinthians 4:5 that when the Lord comes, He "will bring to light the things now hidden in darkness and will disclose the purposes of the heart." Therefore, He'll come during the day.

Thomas responds, echoing Gregory, that Christ's Resurrection is the cause and exemplar of ours. Since Christ rose at night, so shall we. Further, Christ Himself compared the Second Coming to a thief who comes in the night (Luke 12:39–40). Still, Thomas reminds us that we cannot know the exact hour (and Christ could have been speaking figuratively or metaphorically).

As for objections, while time will end, the stars will stay in the same position they occupy naturally at any fixed hour. Though we receive the sun's maximum natural light at midday, the city of God will need neither sun nor moon, "for the Lord God will be their light" (Rev. 22:5). The exact time at which God's light will reveal hidden things is not known to us; therefore, "either

---

[49] "We know neither the moment of the consummation of the earth and of man, nor the way in which the universe will be transformed" (CCC 1048).

[50] *Tempus amplius non erit* in the Latin Bible that Thomas used. Other translations render the verse in different ways. The RSVCE has "There should be no more delay."

may happen fittingly, namely that the resurrection be in the day or in the night."

Will the resurrection happen all at once or be spread out over time?

Some hold that the resurrection will occur gradually, by degrees, since we read in Ezekiel's foretelling of the resurrection that bones, then sinews, flesh, and skin will come together one by one until, breathed on by the Spirit, a great host of people will live and stand again (37:7–10). Thomas replies that the resurrection will happen "in a moment, in the twinkling of an eye" (1 Cor. 15:52). He clarifies that the angels will not collect the matter of our bodies in a single instant, but they *will* perform their ministry so quickly that the human eye could not perceive it. That which is done by God's power—the reunion of soul and body—will indeed happen suddenly at the end of time after the work of the angels, "because the higher power brings the lower to perfection." Thomas further explains that Ezekiel, like Moses before him, was speaking to a "rough people."[51] Both prophets simplified their message so that an uncultured people could understand. Moses divided the work of creation into six days, "although all things were made together according to Augustine," and Ezekiel described the resurrection as a sequence of events, "although they will happen in an instant."

---

[51] *Populi rudi*, meaning an uneducated or unsophisticated population.

14

Ashes to Ashes, Dust to Dust: On Who and What Will Rise Again

The saints differ in speaking on this question. . . .
However, the safer and more common opinion is
that all shall die and rise again from death.

—ST, Supplement, 78, 1

Will those alive at the time of the resurrection
die before they rise again?

It might appear that not all will die before the general resurrection and Last Judgment, for in the Nicene Creed, we declare the Lord will come again in glory "to judge the living and the dead." Further, in the prayer Christ gave us, we pray "forgive us our debts,"[52] and as Christ declared, "If you ask anything of the Father, he will give it to you" (John 16:23). One of our debts is the Original Sin with which we are born. Therefore, at some point, God will allow people to be born without Original Sin. Since death is the punishment of Original Sin, these people will not die.

---

[52] *Dimitte nobis debita nostra*, now translated in English as "forgive us our trespasses."

Thomas responds with 1 Corinthians 15:36, in which Paul says regarding the body, "What you sow does not come to life unless it dies." Further, "as in Adam all die, so also in Christ shall all be made alive" (1 Cor. 15:22). Thomas acknowledges that saints have had differing opinions on the matter, but the most common (and most likely) opinion is that all will arise from death. This is for three main reasons:

1. It makes sense according to divine justice. Because God's justice condemned human nature to death due to sin, it seems that every person who shares in human nature should share the debt of death as well.

2. It is in line with Scripture, which foretells the resurrection of all. As St. John Damascene notes, resurrection refers to that "which has fallen and perished."

3. It is in line with the natural order, according to which "what is corrupted and decayed is not renewed except by means of corruption: thus vinegar does not become wine unless the vinegar be corrupted and pass into the juice of the grape.[53] Wherefore since human nature has incurred the defect of the necessity of death, it cannot return to immortality save by means of death."

The phrase in the Creed about the judgment of the living and the dead refers to the time immediately *before* the judgment, when some signs will begin to appear. We also have no reason to suppose that humans in the future will be born without Original Sin and therefore will not die. God, in His mercy, can forgive

---

[53] The word "vinegar" (*acetum* in Thomas's original Latin) means "sour wine." Today, vinegar is made from wines or sugars when, through a process of fermentation, ethyl alcohol and oxygen chemically react to produce acetic acid.

people for their sins without punishing them, as Christ forgave the adulterer (John 8). If He chose to, He could also forgive the debt of death due to Original Sin. Therefore, even if some people do not die, "it does not follow that … therefore they were born without original sin."

Will everyone rise again from ashes?[54]

We have seen that Christ's Resurrection is the exemplar of ours, yet we read in Acts that God did not let His "Holy One see corruption" (2:27, 31). Further, only some bodies are burned to ashes after death. Lombard has stated that those found living before the judgment will rise again immediately after death, and the body does not turn to ashes immediately after we die.

Thomas responds to these objections by citing Haymo of Halberstadt (778–853), a Benedictine monk and bishop. In a commentary on Romans 5:10, Haymo wrote that "all who are born in original sin lie under the sentence: Earth thou art and into earth thou shalt go." All humans[55] are born in Original Sin, and all will rise again from the ashes. Further, Thomas notes that many things in the human body do not truly belong to human nature,[56] but these will be removed when the body is turned to ash.

---

[54] Because bodies were customarily burned in the past, the word "ashes" is commonly used to refer to all bodily remains, even those that were not burned after death.

[55] Excepting Christ as man, and the Blessed Mother.

[56] We might think, for example, of the microorganisms that live within the human digestive tract and other bodily systems. Some scientists estimate the human body contains *tens of trillions* of microbes such as bacteria, fungi, and viruses.

Thomas explains that just as all will rise *from death*, as we saw in the previous article, all will arise *from ashes*, unless God provides "a special privilege of grace" for some persons in exceptional cases. Like death, the body's decay is a just punishment for sin, as we read in Genesis 3:19: "You are dust and to dust you shall return." When our bodies rise again, Scripture tells us, they will be *reformed* and *glorified*. Christ "will change our lowly body to be like his glorious body" (Phil. 3:21).

In response to objections, Thomas clarifies that "Christ's resurrection is the exemplar of ours as to the term 'whereto,' but not as to the term 'wherefrom.'" In other words, we will be resurrected because of His Resurrection, but not in the same manner. Finally, the fire of the last conflagration, as we saw in chapter 10, will have a special cleansing power that will be able to reduce all living bodies to ashes in an instant, and indeed, to dissolve all other mixed material bodies into their "prejacent" (preexisting) matter.

Will our ashes have a natural inclination to unite with our souls?

Some think that the ashes of a person's body will retain a kind of natural inclination to be reunited to that particular person's soul; otherwise, they would bear the same relation to that soul as any other ashes, and it would not matter whether the soul was united with the ashes of its body or with any ashes whatsoever. Proponents of this belief suppose that within human ashes, there exists a special kind of force or light that gives them a special inclination to reunite with their proper soul.

This is surely an intriguing issue. People have long been aware that humans can be consumed by wild animals, and that even human flesh buried under ground can be consumed by various microorganisms or dissolved into the soil, providing nutrients for plant growth. How, then, can our ashes reunite with our souls? Augustine declares, "The human body, although changed into the substance of other bodies or even into the elements, although it has become the food and flesh of any animals whatsoever, even of man, will in an instant return to that soul which erstwhile animated it, making it a living and growing man."

Thomas responds that for every natural inclination, there is a natural agent to bring it to fruition, but there is no natural power that can reunite a particular person's ashes with his soul. The reunion of body and soul is possible only through the decree of divine providence, by a supernatural act of God.

15

How We Will Regain the Same Body

For the soul, even after separation from the body, retains the
being which accrues to it when in the body, and the body is made
to share that being by the resurrection, since the being of the body
and the being of the soul in the body are not distinct from one
another, otherwise the union of soul and body would be accidental.

—ST, Supplement, 79, 2

Will our souls be reunited with our same bodies?

Scripture seems to suggest that we will not be reunited with our
same bodies at the resurrection. Per 1 Corinthians 15:37, "what
you sow is not the body which is to be, but a bare kernel." Thomas
responds with the clear words of Job. 19:26: "After my skin has
been thus destroyed, then from my flesh I shall see God" on the
Last Day, when the Redeemer will stand on the earth. Further,
per Damascene, "resurrection is the second rising of that which
has fallen." Thomas notes that because the body we have now
fell by death, it will rise again identically.

Thomas elaborates that some philosophers and heretics have
erred greatly in this regard. They argue that not only will we not
reunite with the same body, but also we can be reunited even

with the bodies of other species, so that a lustful person might come back as a dog, a violent person as a lion, and so on. This false opinion comes from two errors: (1) the mistaken belief that the soul and body are not united essentially, as with form and matter, "but only accidentally, as mover to the thing moved ... or as a man to his clothes";[57] and (2) the mistaken belief that the human intellect is not essentially different and superior to the animal powers of sensation, so that it would be possible for a human soul to enter into a brute animal's body. Both mistakes are soundly refuted in Aristotle's *On the Soul*.[58]

1 Corinthians 15:37 does not apply to every particular characteristic, but only to some. The grain sown and the grain reaped are not identical in that grain is sown without a husk and born from the earth with one. The human body that rises again will be identically the same, "but of a different condition, since it was mortal and will rise in immortality."

Will the identically same person rise again?

Doubts about our ability to rise again as the same person arose not from scriptural but philosophical arguments, some buttressed by certain interpretations of Aristotle's writings. He wrote, for

---

[57] Thomas addresses the union of body and soul most thoroughly in the eight articles of *ST*, I, 72, "Of the Union of Body and Soul." We came across this issue briefly in the first section of chapter 13, where we addressed article 1 of *ST*, Supplement, 77, "Of the Time and Manner of the Resurrection."

[58] Thomas provides wonderfully illuminating commentary on every line of that book. See St. Thomas Aquinas, *Commentary on Aristotle's De Anima* (Notre Dame, IN: Dumb Ox Books, 1994).

example, "Whatsoever things are changed in their corruptible substance are not repeated identically." This suggests that man's substance in his present state will be irrevocably corrupted by death.

Thomas responds to the contrary with the words of Scripture. Concerning a vision after the resurrection, Job 19:27 says, "My eyes shall behold, and not another." Thomas then cites Augustine, who wrote that "to rise again is naught else but to live again." Now, unless the same, identical person died to return to life, that person could not be said to live again.

Thomas's own answer begins with a focus on man's ultimate end, or purpose, which is to attain eternal bliss in the Beatific Vision with God in heaven. That is why we were made. Our end cannot be attained in this life on earth, nor cannot it be attained by a separated soul, "otherwise man would have been made in vain, if he were unable to obtain the end for which he was made." This end must be attained by the selfsame person, and this cannot be unless the selfsame soul is reunited with the selfsame body.

As for the objections, Aristotle referred only to natural processes in things subject to generation and corruption. The human soul is spiritual and does not decompose. Further, as we saw in our last chapter, the resurrection results from no natural inclination, but by the power of God's providence.

Will the ashes return to the same parts of the body they came from?

An interesting little question, no? So why was it asked? The first of three objections argues that the ashes *must* return to exactly the same parts of the body that they formed in life, since as Aristotle wrote, "as the whole soul is to the whole body, so is a part of the soul to a part of the body, as sight to the pupil." This would imply that that the parts of the body must return to the same places "in which they were perfected by the same parts of the soul." Another argument holds that through the resurrection, man receives "the meed[59] of his works." Different parts of the body are used for different deeds, warranting merits or demerits, so at the resurrection, each part would need to return to its former place to receive its fitting reward.

Thomas begins by noting that we can reconstruct objects, even artificial, man-made ones, without necessarily placing each part in its exact same position.[60] The same would apply to man. Further, "change of an accident does not cause a change of identity. Now the situation of parts is an accident. Therefore its change in a man does not cause a change of identity."

Thomas's full reply gets a little technical. He distinguishes between *identity* and *congruity*, and between two kinds of parts —those of a *homogeneous* whole and those of a *heterogeneous* whole. Parts of a *homogeneous* whole would include, for example, the various parts of a bone, while the parts of a *heterogeneous* whole differ from each other, as flesh differs from bone. Thomas says the change in the position of parts does not change the identity of *homogeneous* wholes, while it does for *heterogeneous* wholes.

---

[59] A fitting or deserved reward. Thomas's wording is akin to our modern phrase "getting one's just deserts."

[60] If you will forgive the homely first example that comes to this weightlifter's mind, if I were to deadlift 405 pounds two weeks in a row with the same barbell and plates, it would make no difference in which order the eight individual 45-pound plates were arranged on the 45-pound bar from one workout to the next.

A human body is composed of homogeneous and heterogeneous parts, so essential and heterogeneous parts must remain in their same positions, while homogeneous and accidental parts, such as the hair and nails, could change their position without destroying the body's selfsameness, or *identity*. Still, Thomas argues that for that sake of *congruity*, or fittingness, it seems likely that our parts will retain their original positions at the time of the resurrection.

As for certain body *parts* receiving their "meed," Thomas says that rewards are due not to parts, but to the *whole* they form.

16

How Our Hair, Nails, and Bodily Fluids Arise!

The soul is to the animated body,
as art is to the work of art, and is to the parts
of the body as art to its instruments.

—ST, Supplement, 80, 1

Will all parts of the human body arise?
Some believe that not all of the parts of the human body will arise.
We know from Matthew 22:30 that there will be no marriage
in heaven; therefore, there will be no need for the reproductive
organs. Thomas notes, to the contrary, that Lombard explained
that even the hair and nails will be restored, and bodily organs
belong to human nature more than hair and nails. Further, we
know from Deuteronomy 32:4 that all of God's works are perfect.
The resurrection will be a work of God. Therefore, "man will be
remade perfect in all his members."

Thomas elaborates with some fascinating insights from Aristotle on the relationship of the soul and the body. First, "'The
soul stands in relation to the body not only as its form and end,
but also as efficient cause.' For the soul is compared to the body
as art to the thing made by art. In like manner whatever appears

in the parts of the body is all contained originally and, in a way, implicitly in the soul."[61] So too the human being cannot be perfect "unless the whole that is contained enfolded in the soul be outwardly unfolded in the body." Since at the resurrection the human body will correspond entirely to the soul, humans must rise again perfect and complete in all parts of the body.

As to the fact that there will be no marriage or further propagation of the species after the resurrection, the reproductive organs will no longer relate to the soul as an *instrument* to an *agent*, since they will not perform the reproductive function of the soul. That does not mean they will be useless, for they will continue to relate to the soul as *matter* relates to *form*. An instrument exists not only to perform a particular function, but to show the full "virtue" or powers of the soul. The human soul's powers will still be shown through all of its bodily instruments, "even though they never proceed to action, so that the wisdom of God be thereby glorified."

Will our nails and hair arise?

Well, we saw in the answer to our last question that Lombard said they will, and Thomas agreed with him. Still, some disagree for some interesting, if faulty, reasons. For example, nails and hair seem to be superfluities, like urine or sweat, which will not rise again. Further, nothing that has not been perfected by the sensitive soul will receive further perfection from the rational soul.

---

[61] Indeed, while many modern philosophers and psychologists wonder how a spiritual soul (or at least a "mind") can arise from a material body, Aristotle and Thomas hold that *one of the soul's most fundamental acts is to grow the appropriate body!*

Hair and nails are not perfected by the sensitive soul because, as Aristotle notes, we do not feel with them.

Thomas counters with the clear words of Luke 21:18: "Not a hair of your head will perish." Further, Thomas notes that the hair and nails are given to humans as adornments, and we ought to rise again with all our adornments. The hair and nails also play important roles under the soul's direction. While some bodily organs or members, such as the heart, the hand, and the foot, serve the organic whole through *direct operations* or *actions*, other parts of the body, such as the hair and nails, play a *safeguarding role* for the other parts, as leaves serve to protect and cover fruit. Therefore, while hair and nails do not contribute to the *primary* perfection of the human body, they do contribute to the *secondary* perfection, and will rise again in the resurrected body.

As for the objections, superfluities, such as urine or sweat, are voided by nature and serve no further protective or adorning function, as do hair and nails. Further, the human being has but one soul, which possesses rational as well as sensitive and vegetative powers. Since hair and nails grow, they are in some way perfected by the powers of the human soul. That we do not feel with them is irrelevant, since bones, for example, do not function as sense organs, yet they will rise again.

Will our blood and bodily fluids arise?

We read in 1 Corinthians 15:50 that "flesh and blood cannot inherit the kingdom of God." Since blood is the chief bodily humor,[62] some people believe that no humors will be found in

---

[62] The four bodily "humors" described in classical and medieval times were blood, yellow bile, black bile, and phlegm.

the resurrected body. Further, some argue that the body's humors are involved in the processing of bodily waste, and after the resurrection, there will be no waste.

Thomas answers, to the contrary, that whatever is part of the human body's constitution will rise again with it. Augustine wrote (according to the biological understanding of his day) that "the body consists of functional members; the functional members of homogeneous parts; and the homogeneous parts of humors." Therefore, Thomas notes, the humors will arise with the body. Further, our resurrection will conform to Christ's. We know His blood rose again, for indeed, if it had not, "the wine would not now be changed into His blood in the Sacrament of the altar." So our blood and other humors will also arise.

As for 1 Corinthians 15:50, the Apostle's words do not describe the *substance* of flesh and blood, but the *deeds* of flesh and blood that relate to sin or to functions of animal life. We may also conclude, with Augustine, that Paul is referring specifically to the perishable *corruption* of flesh and blood, since he concludes the same verse with the words "Nor does the perishable inherit the imperishable."[63]

Will everything in the body that is essential
human nature arise? (Or, what about the cannibals?)

Thomas declares that "whatever belonged to the truth of human nature was perfected by the rational soul. Now it is through being perfected by the rational soul that the human body is directed to the resurrection. Therefore whatever belonged to the truth

---

[63] Thomas's Latin Bible uses the words *corruptio* and *incorruptionem*, translated in the RSVCE as "perishable" and "imperishable."

of human nature will rise again." Whatever is essential to our human nature will rise again; otherwise, our bodies would not be perfect (which also means "complete") after the resurrection.

These statements from Thomas's "On the contrary" section seem rather straightforward and logical. So where does this business about cannibals come in?

In this article, Thomas presents four objections. The first states that most likely not everything in the body that belonged to the truth of human nature (of essentially *human* nature) will rise again. Sometimes, for example, we eat the flesh of other animals, such as cows, as food, and it does not make sense to say that the flesh of other animals will rise again. Thomas answers this objection pretty readily by noting that what is natural to a thing comes from its *form* and not its *matter*, so that "although that part of matter which at one time was under the form of bovine flesh rises again in man under the form of human flesh, it does not follow that the flesh of an ox rises again, but the flesh of a man: else one might conclude that the clay from which Adam's body was fashioned shall rise again."

It is in the third, fourth, and fifth objections that cannibals are mentioned and the analysis of the issue becomes most intriguing. The third objection holds that it is impossible for the same matter from different people to arise again, and yet it is possible for matter from different people to belong to the truth of a single person's human nature. If a human were to consume another person's flesh, that flesh would be changed into the substance of the cannibal. Therefore, what belonged to the truth of that first person's human nature would not arise in him. In an even more bizarre thought experiment, the fourth objection considers the case of a child of a man who ate nothing but human flesh. Even the seed that produced the child would have come through the flesh of other human beings. Therefore, whatever belongs to the truth of that child's human nature was first possessed by others.

Thomas considers several different opinions in responding to these objections. I'll present here the briefest and most straightforward. In the case of a cannibal, human flesh that is eaten never belonged to the cannibal in the truth of his human nature, but belonged to the person who was eaten. Therefore, it will rise in the person eaten, and not the cannibal. As to the fourth objection, Thomas replies that human seed is not produced by the surplus of food that a man eats, so "the flesh eaten is not changed into the seed whereof the child is begotten."

Will whatever was inside our bodies arise?

To get to the heart of the matter, Thomas's answer is no, and he notes early in a rather understated way that "all the matter that was in a man from the beginning of his life to the end would surpass the quantity due to his species." (Indeed, just think how much food we take in over the course of a lifetime and how frequently our bodies replace and renew our cells. One can hardly imagine how huge we would be at the resurrection if *all* that matter was restored to us!) Thomas clarifies that everything that belongs to "the truth of human nature" in terms of the quantity, shape, position, or order of parts will arise, but the totality of all the matter that was ever in the human body will not.

17

What Our Bodies Will Be Like
at the Resurrection

Man will rise again without any defect of human nature,
because as God founded human nature without a
defect, even so will He restore it without defect.

—ST, Supplement, 81, 1

How old will we be when we arise?

This is certainly an intriguing issue, since people may die at any
stage of life, from infancy to extreme old age. Some believe,
therefore, that people will arise at different ages. The elderly, for
example, will not arise as youths, because aging helps perfect a
person (which is why we show reverence to older people). God
would not remove their perfection. Others argue that if all were
to arise at the same age, it should be as children, since children
carry the truth of human nature, and as we age, parts of the body
become weakened. Indeed, Aristotle likened the aging body to
watery wine.

Thomas begins by citing Ephesians 4:13, which tells us that
we are charged with building up the Body of Christ "until we
all attain to the unity of the faith and of the knowledge of the

Son of God, to mature manhood, to the measure of the stature of the fulness of Christ." Thomas notes that Christ rose again at a youthful age, which begins around thirty, according to Augustine. This is also the most perfect stage of human nature.[64] Therefore, all will arise at that age.

Thomas elaborates that we will arise without any defects, and human nature, as it is now, possesses a "twofold defect." Children possess a defect in that they have not yet attained their ultimate physical perfection, and the aged possess a defect in that they have declined from their ultimate perfection. Therefore, the perfected body of the resurrection will be of a youthful condition of ultimate perfection, the point at which growth has ended and decline has not yet occurred.

Thomas notes as well that *the aged are rightly revered, not on account of their bodies, but on account of the soul's wisdom.* Therefore, *even when resurrected in youthful bodies, those who attained old age will still be revered* "on account of the fulness of Divine wisdom which will be in them, but the defect of old age will

---

[64] As a hopefully interesting aside, I decided to do a little Internet search for the phrase "peak age for athletic performance." Results on the first page included mention of the fact that though there are differences of a few years here and there depending on the sport, both endurance (as evidenced by the performance of marathon runners) and measured muscle mass peak *at around age thirty!* See Ross Pomeroy, "This Is When Athletes Hit Their Peak," Real Clear Science, June 24, 2015, https://www.realclearscience. com/journal_club/2015/06/25/this_is_when_athletes_hit_their_ peak_109280.html, and John A. Batsis and Silvio Buscemi, "Sarcopenia, Sarcopenic Obesity and Insulin Resistance," in *Medical Complications of Type 2 Diabetes*, ed. Colleen Croniger (Rijeka, Croatia: InTech, 2011), 236, https://www.researchgate. net/figure/Muscle-Mass-Changes-with-Aging-Peak-muscle-mass- occurs-between-the-ages-of-20-and-30_fig3_221916428.

not be in them." As for children, while their bodies do possess the greatest powers of growth, they have not yet attained the ultimate perfection found in youthful maturity, which is the age at which all will arise.

Will we all be the same height?

Some think that since we will all be restored at the same age — a quantity of time — so too will we all be restored at the same stature — a quantity of dimension. Thomas responds that neither an individual's nature nor his natural quantity will be altered at the resurrection. Since natural quantities differ between persons, everyone will *not* rise again of the same stature.

Thomas observes the parallel case that while some bodies will be restored to obtain glory and others to receive punishment, the quantity or degree of glory and punishment will vary from person to person. *The resurrection restores not only human nature in general, but the individual nature of every unique person.*

Still, if a person in life had some kind of defect that stunted or accelerated his physical growth below or beyond the perfection of nature, making him exceedingly small or large, then at the resurrection, God's divine power will remedy the defect to perfect that person's human nature.

Will we remain male and female at the resurrection?

Misinterpretations of Scripture and erroneous ancient and medieval understandings of human reproduction led some to believe that all would rise again as males. Proponents of this idea cited Ephesians 4:13, which states we will arise when we attain "mature manhood," and 1 Corinthians 15:24, which declares that

God the Father will destroy "every rule and every authority and power." A medieval gloss on the latter held that since women are subject to men in the natural order, they will not remain female at the resurrection.[65] Finally, some cited Aristotle, who wrote that the female sex is a defective state that results when there is a fault in the formative power of the male seed, so that it does not produce the male sex that nature intends.

Thomas begins by citing Augustine, who wrote that wise people do not doubt that both sexes will rise again. Further, God will restore man to his original created state: male (as He created Adam) and female (as He created Eve). Thomas elaborates that the diversity of the sexes "is becoming to the perfection of the species." When St. Paul wrote that all will meet Christ in "mature manhood," he meant not as members of the male sex, but in the perfect strength of the soul that all will possess, both men and women. As for women's being subject to men on earth, Thomas believed that women have a relative frailty according to nature, but after the resurrection, the only differences that will matter will be based on "the difference of merits" that men and women earned as individuals.

As for the last point, I will note that Thomas greatly respected the authority of Aristotle and did not possess modern scientific

---

[65] Quite interestingly, the second-century Gnostic Gospel of St. Thomas, purportedly a collection of secret sayings of Jesus, has intrigued some modern proponents of New Age beliefs. In the final saying of that book, Peter tells Jesus to leave Mary because "women are not worthy of life," to which Jesus responds that He would make her a male, since "every woman who will make herself male will enter the kingdom of heaven." It should not surprise readers that the ancient Church recognized in an instant that this book was in no way inspired Scripture.

knowledge of chromosomes and other factors of human reproduction that determine sex. Still, when using physical examples from the scientific knowledge of his day to illustrate philosophical or theological principles in the *Summa*, Thomas acknowledged that those scientific beliefs might later be found in error as further knowledge accrues. Moreover, even in this particular case, founded upon the faulty biological understanding of the time, Thomas makes the very reasonable point that even if, in an individual case, the conception of a woman is beside the intention of a particular, individual nature, "it is in the intention of universal nature, which requires both sexes for perfection of the human species." Therefore, the perfected female at the resurrection will in no way be defective or inferior.

Will all arise with the animal functions of nutrition and generation?

Some believe that when we arise, our bodies will possess both nutritive and generative powers. As Christ ate after His Resurrection (John 21, Luke 24), so will we. We will retain our other natural powers, too, such as those of reproduction. Others note that the use of our nutritive and reproductive powers provides us with great pleasures. Boethius (ca. 480–ca. 525) wrote that happiness "is a state rendered perfect by the accumulation of all goods." Therefore, we will not be deprived of such goods.

Thomas replies that Matthew 22:30 clearly states that we will not marry, but will be like angels. Reproduction is necessary now on earth "to supply the defect resulting from death," and to multiply the population, but at the resurrection, humans will have reached the number God preordained, and there will be no new births. As for nourishment, it makes up for the loss of matter through waste and provides for new growth, but after the resurrection, the human body will be perfected and will not require natural animal functions to sustain it. Thomas concludes that natural functions, such as eating, drinking, sleeping, and begetting, which serve only the natural perfection of the body, will no longer be needed, since we will have reached our ultimate perfection.

Christ ate and drank after His Resurrection, not out of necessity, but to prove to His disciples that He retained His human nature. There will clearly be no need for such proof when Christ appears again to all at the general resurrection. As for the pleasures of food and sexual union, Thomas notes that while some people, including certain Jews, Saracens (Muslims), and chiliasts (millennialists) of the day understood heaven or paradise as filled with *bodily* pleasures, even the pagan Aristotle recognized that the simplest, purest, and highest pleasures are *spiritual*. These pleasures are sought for their own sake and are *sufficient for complete happiness or beatitude*.

18

Ultimate Athletes for Christ:
Impassible Glorified Bodies

*Now the human body and all that it contains will be
perfectly subject to the rational soul, even as the soul will
be perfectly subject to God. Wherefore it will be impossible
for the glorified body to be subject to any change contrary
to the disposition whereby it is perfected by the soul;
and consequently those bodies will be impassible.*

—*ST*, Supplement, 82, 1

Will our bodies in heaven be impassible?
(And what is impassibility, anyway?)

Impassibilis, per Thomas, means "incapable of suffering." Some
hold that impassibility is not possible for man, whom wise philosophers defined as a "mortal rational animal." Any mortal
being is subject to suffering, pain, and decomposition. Thomas
responds that we know the glorified body will not deteriorate:
"What is sown is perishable, what is raised is imperishable" (1
Cor. 15:42). Further, a stronger thing is not vulnerable to the
weaker, and no body will be stronger than the bodies of the
saints, of which we read: "It is sown in weakness, it is raised in

127

power" (1 Cor. 15:43). Therefore, the bodies of the saints will be impassible.

Now, "passible" can mean, broadly speaking, "capable of receiving or being altered by things." The glorified body will not be impassible in that sense, since it will retain the human capacity of receiving perfections, as when we receive information from the outside world throughout senses. But, in a more specific sense, "passible" can mean "capable of being affected by the passions." According to St. John Damascene, a passion is "a movement contrary to nature." In this sense, an immoderate, abnormal movement of the heart is called a *passion*, while a normal, moderate movement is called its *operation*. The glorified body will be invulnerable to immoderate responses of any kind. It will perform its perfected operations without inappropriate passions.

In our life on earth after the Fall and the entrance of sin into human nature, we can have great difficulty using our reason to regulate our emotional passions regarding things that we love or hate. (We might think of the tug-of-war many of us experience, with the intellect and the will on one side and the passions on the other, when it comes to disciplining ourselves to get the exercise our bodies need and to keep from eating and drinking potentially harmful things.) Yet after the resurrection, "the human body and all that it contains will be perfectly subject to the rational soul, even as the soul will be perfectly subject to God." Indeed, we will experience "the triumph of the soul over the body."[66]

---

[66] I cannot help but note parallels here with the ideas and goals of the ancient Stoic philosophers. They held up an ideal of *apatheia*, which means "without passion" or a state in which

As for the "mortal rational animal," Thomas cites St. Anselm of Canterbury (1033–1109), who noted that the ancient philosophers included the word "mortal" in their definition of man "because they did not believe that the whole man could be ever immortal, for they had no experience of man otherwise than in this state of mortality." Thomas clarifies that the word "mortal" is not essential to the definition of man, because mortality is essential to man only in our state of life here on earth while we are passible and vulnerable to corruption.

Thomas concludes with another intriguing insight on the impassibility of the glorified body. The saints who suffered scars for the Faith, such as some of the martyrs, will still bear those scars, as Christ did when He rose from the tomb. Yet, as Augustine notes, the scars will not appear as defects. All in heaven will know how the saints earned those scars, which will actually add to their comeliness or beauty. Those who were maimed or lost limbs, however, will have them restored, in keeping with the body's perfection, as it is said in Luke 21:18: "Not a hair of your head will perish."

---

one's reason would rule one's passions. In this state, one would never be overcome by negative emotions, such as anger, worry, depression, lust, and so on. Some, such as Epictetus (ca. A.D. 50–135), even stated that such *apatheia* meant that one's will would be fully aligned with God's will. They declared that a true sage would achieve this state. Still, grasping the gist of human nature, but unaware of Christ, they declared that while some, such as Socrates, had come close to this state, no one had ever fully attained it. How fascinating that, in a sense, all of us who are graced with a glorified body in heaven will have attained the seemingly impossible goal of the impassible Stoic sage!

Will all bodies be impassible to the same extent?

Though all of the blessed in heaven will enjoy impassibility, rewards should be proportionate to merit, meaning that saints who have merited greater rewards will experience greater impassibility. Impassibility in the sense of a *negation* or *privation* of the experience of suffering *will be the same* for us all in heaven, but as to its *cause*, impassibility arises from the soul's dominion over the body, which in turn is caused by "the soul's unchangeable enjoyment of God." Therefore, the saints who can more fully experience the joy of God will have a greater cause of their impassibility.

Will our impassible bodies possess the capacity for sensation?

Since, per Aristotle, "sensation is a kind of passion," some believe we will no longer possess our five senses in our glorified bodies, but we read in Scripture that "every eye will see" Jesus when He comes again (Rev. 1:7). Therefore, we shall indeed regain sight when reunited with our bodies at the resurrection. Aristotle notes that sensation and movement are intertwined in living things, and we read in Scripture that we will be able to move in heaven—we "will run like sparks through the stubble" (Wisd. 3:7). Indeed, there will be sensation in the bodies of the blessed, "else the bodily life of the saints after the resurrection would be likened to sleep rather than to vigilance."

Will all impassible bodies possess all five powers of sensation?

Some believe certain senses will be lacking in the glorified body. Taste, for example, assists in nourishment, a function that will no longer take place. Similarly, smell requires a kind of corruption or evaporation of substances, and there will be no corruption after the resurrection. Thomas responds, however, that human nature will be completely perfected in the blessed, and all the senses will remain and become perfected. Further, not only the soul but also the body will receive its rewards or punishments, and this requires sensation.

19

The Subtlety of Our Glorified Bodies

The more subtle a body is the more exalted it is.
But the glorified bodies will be most exalted.
Therefore they will be most subtle.

—*ST*, Supplement, 83, 1

Will our glorified bodies possess subtlety?
(And just what is subtlety?)

Thomas declares that *subtilitas* (subtlety) "takes its name from the power to penetrate," and our glorified bodies will possess such penetrative power, as did the resurrected body of Christ when He suddenly vanished and appeared before His disciples, as described in the last chapter of Luke's Gospel. Some think this impossible, because only things with less matter can penetrate denser things. For instance, water can penetrate things that earth cannot, and fire can penetrate what even air cannot. We know that our glorified bodies will have the same quantity of matter as our earthly bodies. According to Gregory, certain heretics said that our glorified bodies will be rarefied and become like air, wind, or pure spirit, yet we know this is false. We will possess real flesh and bone. Christ Himself declared, "See my hands and my feet, that it is I myself; handle me, and see; for a spirit has not flesh and bones as you see that I have" (Luke 24:39). Job 19:26 also tells us, "From my flesh I shall see God."

We read of the glorified body in 1 Corinthians 15:44: "It is sown a physical body, it is raised a spiritual body. If there is a physical body, there is also a spiritual body." Thomas explains that we will obtain a spirit-like body. It will be composed of real flesh and blood, but like spiritual substances, it will possess the ability to penetrate material objects. This is neither because our bodies will resemble wind or fire nor because we will be pure spirit. Instead, it is because God will grant our bodies such complete perfection that not only will the soul possess total dominion over the passions to such an extent, as we have seen, that we will be *impassible*, but also the body will be *spiritual* in the sense that it will be so completely subject to the spirit, our matter so completely subject to our form, that it will attain the capacity to move where we will, and this is what we call *subtlety*. Thus Gregory states that "the glorified body is said to be subtle as a result of a spiritual power."

Can a glorified body, because of its subtlety, be in the same place as a non-glorified body?

Perhaps this question already occurred to you (or perhaps not!). In any event, Thomas provides a full five arguments from people who believe the answer is yes. One of these objections derives from the fact that Christ, in His glorified body, was able to pass through locked doors and appear to His disciples (John 20:19, 26). Thomas provides very lengthy philosophical, mathematical, and indeed *subtle* (in the sense of difficult and nuanced) arguments from Aristotle and Boethius to the contrary. For example,

Boethius writes that "we cannot possibly conceive two bodies occupying one place." Thomas notes that even a subtle body will occupy space. Indeed, in his clarification of the meaning of "subtlety" in the first question of this chapter, he cited Aristotle, who wrote that "a subtle thing fills all the parts and the parts of parts." A subtle body will fill a space, and indeed, "it would seem madness to say that the place in which there will be a glorified body will be empty."

As for Christ's walking through doors, Thomas clarifies that this was not due to His subtlety, but to the power of His Godhead. Gregory notes that it was by this same power that Christ "came from the closed womb of the Virgin at His birth." Further, we should recall that Peter had the power to heal the sick who merely passed through his shadow (Acts 5:15), but this was not due to any power inherent in his body, but to the divine power of God, "for the upbuilding of the faith. Thus will the Divine power," not the quality of subtlety alone, "make it possible for a glorified body to be in the same place together with another body for the perfection of glory."

Is it possible by a miracle for two bodies to be in the same place?

Perhaps you have gathered from our last question that Thomas's answer is yes, as long as we pay special heed to the qualifying words "by a miracle." He cites two examples from our last section, namely, the Virgin Birth and Christ's walking through doors. These were done through special acts of God's divine power — that is, miracles. The presence of two distinct bodies in the same place is another instance of something that can never occur naturally, but through God's power alone, as happens in when "it is possible for an accident to be without substance as in the Sacrament of the Altar."

Can one glorified body be in the same place as another glorified body?

Some hold that two glorified bodies, through their extreme powers of penetration, could share the same place. Thomas answers, citing Lombard, that the glorified body will be spiritual and like a spirit in some respect, and while a body and spirit can share the same place, no two spirits can share the same place. "Therefore neither will two glorified bodies be able to be in the same place." If two glorified bodies shared the same space, they would penetrate one another. This would be a mark of imperfection. Glorified bodies are perfect and demand distinction from one another. Again, it would require a miraculous act of God's divine power for a glorified body to share the same space with either a non-glorified or a glorified body.

Can a glorified body occupy a space of a different size?

Some argue that due to its subtlety, the glorified body will be able to occupy a space of a different size, just as the whole body of Christ is contained in a consecrated host. Thomas begins his response with the words of Aristotle that "whatever is in a place occupies a place equal to itself." The dimensions of a given space and that which fills it are the same, so in order for a space to be larger than what fills it, "the same thing would be greater and smaller than itself, which is absurd." This logical contradiction points to an utterly impossible event that "will never happen, not even by a miracle." Even with His divine power, God does not make false, impossible things true.

As for the objections, Thomas explains that "Christ's body is not locally in the Sacrament of the Altar."[67]

Will our glorified bodies be palpable?

Gregory reports that Eutychius (512–582), bishop of Constantinople, espoused the heretical opinion that glorified bodies would be impalpable, that is, untouchable. Thomas responds that Christ made it clear that His resurrected body could be touched and felt, and He invited His disciples to "handle" Him (Luke 24:39). (Indeed, did not Thomas's namesake place his hand in Christ's

---

[67] As Thomas explained in his discussion of the Sacrament of the Eucharist, Christ's Body, Blood, Soul, and Divinity are *sacramentally* present by God's power through the process of *transubstantiation* in a manner that exceeds the limits of our understanding. While the *substance* of the bread and wine is transformed into Christ's Body, Blood, Soul, and Divinity, the bread and wine retain their *accidents*—that is, how they appear to the eye—including the "dimensive quantity" of size. While retaining the accidents of their own nature, the bread and wine miraculously receive "the power and property of substance; and therefore it can pass to both, that is, into substance and dimension" (*ST*, III, 77, 5).

Here's a modern analogy that I hope will help. In the sacrament of the Eucharist, God does not act like a zip file, compacting Christ's physical properties within the molecules of the bread and wine. Rather, through God's limitless power over all corporeal things, Christ's substance—His Body, Blood, Soul, and Divinity—becomes sacramentally (not locally or physically) present in the bread and wine without altering their accidents, such as their chemical composition, color, taste, and—most relevant to our point—size. Transubstantiation infinitely exceeds the capability of even a glorified fully human body, and so we will not be able to occupy spaces in this way.

wounded side?) Thomas replies that our glorified bodies, though subtle and completely capable of moving however our spirit directs, will indeed not only be palpable, but will add to our bliss: "The touch of those bodies will be most delightful, because a power always delights in a becoming object."

20

Our Gloriously Agile New Bodies

*Wherefore even as by the gift of subtlety the body is
wholly subject to the soul as its form, whence it derives
its specific being, so by the gift of agility it is subject to the
soul as its mover, so that it is prompt and apt to obey the
spirit in all the movements and actions of the soul.*

—*ST*, Supplement, 84, 1

Will our bodies possess agility?
(And what does "agility" mean here?)

Some believe the glorified body will not receive perfected agility
of movement. A gloss on 1 Thessalonians 4:16 indicates that
our glorified bodies will be carried up into the clouds by angels
to meet Christ, which would suggest that our bodies will not be
perfect in their own movements.

Thomas responds with 1 Corinthians 15:43, which says of the
body, "It is sown in weakness, it is raised in power." He reports
that according to a gloss, this verse means our glorified bodies
will be "living and mobile," with "mobile" meaning "having ease
or agility in movement." As we see in our opening quotation, as
subtlety reflects the subjection of the body to the soul as its *form*,

agility reflects the subjection of the body to the soul as its *mover*; hence, our movements will be perfected and performed with ease. This is certainly good news for anyone who has begun to suffer loss of bodily function due to the physical deterioration of aging or injury. Further, consider the hope the passage below offers to those who have struggled to control their bodily movements, such as athletes, who must practice their skills again and again before they become smooth, efficient, effortless, and effective:

> The more the power of the moving soul dominates over the body, the less is the labor of movement, even though it be counter to the body's nature. Hence those in whom the motive power is stronger, and those who through exercise have the body more adapted to obey the moving spirit, labor less in being moved.

This means, Thomas says, that "there will be no labor in the saints' movements, and thus it may be said that the bodies of the saints will be agile." Moreover, the gift of agility will also perfect our powers of sensation and the execution of all bodily operations under the power of the soul. In this sense, all in heaven will, indeed, become agile athletes for Christ! If we are to be borne by the angels to meet Christ in the clouds, this is not because we will need their aid, but in order to display the reverence that the angels (and in fact all creatures) will have for glorified human saints!

Will we use our power of agility to move from place to place?

Some people believe we will not move about in heaven because, as Aristotle stated, "movement is the act of the imperfect," and

Augustine stated that when the soul and body are established in God's will, neither soul nor body will ever move away from Him.[68]

To the contrary, Thomas cites the words of Isaiah 40:31 — "They shall run and walk and not be weary, they shall walk and not faint" — and Wisdom 3:7 — "They ... will run like sparks through the stubble." Even Christ's body was moved in His Ascension; likewise, the bodies of saints "ascend to the empyrean." Thomas argues that even after their ascension, the saints will move about as they please to utilize the gift of agility God has given to them to display "the excellence of Divine wisdom." Further, he argues that our vision will be refreshed by viewing the variety of creatures, which will all reflect God's wisdom, and which will shine forth more brightly than while here on earth. Though the vision of the saints will become more powerful, allowing them to see things at greater distances, they will also have the capacity to move closer to objects of beauty. Such movements will not diminish their happiness consisting in the Beatific Vision of God, because "He will be everywhere present to them; thus Gregory says of the angels ... that 'wherever they are sent their course lies in God.'"

As for Aristotle's statement on the imperfection of movement, this will apply to all living things, even the glorified human body, for only God can rest in all places at once. Still, such a defect is not inconsistent with the perfection of human nature, which includes the capacity to move from place to place. As for Augustine's statement, the glorified body's movement will not move it away from God, but will demonstrate the glorified soul's power, received as a gift from God.

---

[68] We might recall here one of Augustine's most famous sayings about God, found in his *Confessions*: "Our heart is restless until it rests in you."

Will our glorified bodies move instantaneously?

Using modern superhero language, we could rephrase this question as "Will we become faster than the Flash?" Some think that, due to the enhanced spiritual powers of the glorified soul, the glorified body will move instantaneously, passing from one place to another without any passage of time, just as the will passes from one place to the next without passing through intervals in between. Indeed, Thomas provides five objections and notes that opinions are quite divided on this issue.

He concludes, however, that such views do not hold. He wrote elsewhere[69] that angels, when they have not assumed a physical body for some special task from God, can move from one place to another without moving through the points in between, but this is because they are purely spiritual beings, without physical bodies. The glorified body, however, "will never attain to the dignity of the spiritual nature, just as it will never cease to be a body." Thomas then provides a very detailed explanation of how physical bodies move through space, demonstrating that the instantaneous movement of physical bodies "is impossible since it implies a contradiction." I will skip those details and cut to the chase. Thomas concludes that it is most *probable* that while our glorified bodies will move in time, their agility may make the time it takes to move them so small as to be imperceptible. It would seem, then, that Thomas believes that we will indeed be able to move as fast as (or perhaps even faster than) the Flash. In fact, we will move like "sparks," you will recall, according to Wisdom 3:7!

[69] *ST*, I, 53, 2.

21

Seeking Mental Clarity about Bodily Clarity

*The glory of the body will not destroy nature but will
perfect it. . . . Thus we see bodies which have color by
their nature aglow with the resplendence of the sun,
or from some other cause extrinsic or intrinsic.*

—ST, Supplement, 85, 1

Will glorified bodies possess clarity?
(And what is clarity, anyway?)

By the *claritas* of the glorified body, Thomas refers to its beautiful
clearness, radiant brilliance, and *lucidum* (lightsomeness). Some
think that glorified bodies cannot possess clarity for several reasons.
For one, the Persian philosopher Avicenna (980–1037) stated that
"every luminous body consists of transparent parts," but the glorified
body will not be transparent, because it consists of nontransparent
parts, such as flesh and bone. Others cite Aristotle, who argued that
light characterizes the extreme visibility of an *indeterminate body,*
while *color* determines the extreme point of visibility in a *determinate
body.* Augustine, too, wrote that "the body's beauty is a harmony
of parts with a certain charm of color." Since the perfected body
cannot lack beauty, it must possess color and cannot be lightsome.

Thomas begins his response with the words of Matthew 13:43: "The righteous will shine like the sun in the kingdom of their Father." Further, the verse "It is sown in dishonor, it is raised in glory" (1 Cor. 15:43) refers to clarity, because it follows a passage on the glory of luminous celestial bodies. The glorified body will be radiant or lightsome and will also possess a manner of transparency. Indeed, "in the glorified body the glory of the soul will be known, even as through a crystal is known the color of a body contained in a crystal vessel, as Gregory says on Job 28:17, 'Gold or crystal cannot equal it.'"

As for Avicenna's statement on luminosity and transparency, he is referring to bodies that have clarity because of the nature of their component parts. The glorified body will not have clarity because of its parts, "but rather by merit of virtue … that glorified body will have clarity." As for Aristotle and Augustine's comments, Thomas replies: "The glory of the body will not destroy nature but will perfect it." The body will retain the beauty of its colors due to the nature of its component parts, but will also receive clarity due to the soul's glory, as when we now see bodies with color by their nature "aglow with the resplendence of the sun, or from some other cause extrinsic or intrinsic."[70]

---

[70] As for "intrinsic" causation, we might think of the astonishingly beautiful luminous and transparent sea creatures that produce light within themselves through biochemical processes, a phenomenon known as bioluminescence. Indeed, modern scientists have determined that human beings, like all other living beings, *do* emit light arising from chemical reactions occurring within our bodies. This light is far too weak to be seen by human eyes, but as Thomas makes clear, this light will shine brilliantly for all to see when we possess gloriously clarified bodies!

Will the clarity of the glorified body be visible to the non-glorified eye?

Some think the clarity of the glorified body will be completely invisible to those with non-glorified bodies. Consider, for example, that with our non-glorified bodies, we are unable to stare at the sun because of the power of its clarity. We read in Isaiah 30:26 that after the resurrection, the light of the sun will be seven times greater. Our glorified bodies will shine brighter than even the sun, so no non-glorified body will be able to gaze upon them.

Thomas answers with a gloss on Philippians 3:21, which declares that Christ "will change our lowly body to be like his glorious body." The gloss states that the glorified will possess the clarity Christ had at His Transfiguration.[71] This clarity was visible to His non-glorified apostles. Further, one of the torments of the wicked will be to see the glory of the just (Wisd. 5:2).

Thomas concludes that that glorified body will be visible to the non-glorified eye without the need for a miracle. As for the brightness of the sun, while its light and heat can destroy the organ of sight, the intense clarity of the glorified body will be of a different sort, arising from the actions not of matter, but of the spiritual soul. This kind of "intense clarity does not disturb the sight, in so far as it acts by the action of the soul, for thus it rather gives delight." Indeed, though the clarity of the glorified body will exceed that of the sun, it will not disturb, but actually soothe the sight. This is why the clarity of the heavenly Jerusalem is compared to jasper: "Having the glory of God, its radiance like a most rare jewel, like a jasper, clear as crystal" (Rev. 21:11).

---

[71] See Matthew 17:1–8, Mark 9:2–8, Luke 9:28–36, and 2 Peter 1:16–18.

Will a glorified body necessarily be
seen be a non-glorified eye?

It might seem that glorified bodies, which are capable of being seen by non-glorified eyes, will *always* be visible to them. Bodies that emit light, after all, reveal both themselves and other things, as we see in the case of the sun and its light.

Thomas, however, disagrees. He offers a rather amazing conclusion, declaring that, if you'll forgive another fictional reference, our glorified bodies will possess not only the speed of the Flash, but the amazing power of the Invisible Man! You see, the glorified body will be completely obedient to the power of the will: "Therefore as the soul lists the body will be visible or invisible." And how does Thomas arrive at this conclusion? Our bodies will be glorified like Christ's, and we see in Luke 24:31 that Christ could appear to His disciples or vanish from their sight at will. Truly, the power of clarity is a most awesome gift to look forward to!

22

On the Sorry State of the Bodies of the Damned

There will be nothing in the damned to lessen the sense of pain.

—*ST*, Supplement, 86, 1

Will the damned rise again with any bodily deformities they may have suffered?

Some believe the damned will rise again with any deformities they may have suffered, such as the loss of limbs or bodily damage due to illness, since this would contribute to their just punishment for their sins. Thomas responds with words of Scripture: "The dead will be raised imperishable" (1 Cor. 15:52). A gloss explains that all the dead, including sinners, will arise without the loss of any limbs. Thomas adds that destroyed tissues and missing limbs would keep pain from affecting the whole body, and the damned are to suffer all throughout their bodies.

Thomas distinguishes two kinds of deformity: those involving the loss of limbs, and those involving the destruction of tissues due to various sicknesses or illnesses. He declares that lost limbs will no doubt be restored for both the damned and the just, since all bodies will be made whole at the resurrection. Concerning the other kind of deformities that might arise from fevers or other ailments, he notes that we cannot be sure. Lombard tells

147

us that even Augustine remained undecided and doubtful about the matter, and Thomas reports that among "modern masters" there are two opinions. Some hold that deformities of the latter kind will remain in the damned, with no affliction removed that would diminish their utmost unhappiness.

Thomas provides a nuanced argument that casts doubt on such an opinion. He asks us to imagine two sinners who are to be damned, one a most heinous sinner who never suffered bodily deformity, and a second with fewer grievous sins who had suffered deformities of illness. It would be unjust for the deformities of the lesser sinner to remain, because "the mode of the punishment would not correspond to the amount of guilt; in fact it would seem that a man is more punished on account of the pains which he suffered in the world; which is absurd."

The more likely conclusion is that God, who made us whole in nature, will likewise restore us whole, without any physical deformities, including those of the second kind, such as blindness or deafness. Defects that are natural to human bodies, such as their heaviness, passibility (susceptibility to suffering), and so forth, will remain in the bodies of the damned, but will be "removed from the bodies of the elect by the glory of the resurrection."

Will the bodies of the damned be corruptible and subject to disintegration?

One of the most interesting arguments supporting the idea that the bodies of the damned *will* be susceptible to corruption holds that nature, grace, or glory would be necessary for the bodies of the damned to be incorruptible. It cannot be by nature, since natural bodies do deteriorate, and it cannot be by grace or glory, since the damned will lack both.

Thomas responds, to the contrary, with the clear words of Revelation 9:6: "And in those days men will seek death and will not find it; they will long to die, and death will fly from them." Further, the damned will be punished eternally, both in soul and body: "They will go away into eternal punishment" (Matt. 25:46). This could not happen if their bodies were perishable; therefore, their bodies will be incorruptible. While it is true that this incorruptibility will not arise from grace or glory, *it will indeed arise from nature*, not in the sense that their bodies will be incorruptible by *their own* nature, but because *the natural processes that corrupt bodies* will have ceased to operate.

Will the bodies of the damned be impassible like those of the saints?

Augustine asserted that the bodies of the damned will not be consumed by the fires of hell. Therefore, it seems that their bodies, like those of the blessed, will suffer no distress, because like the bodies of the blessed, they will be impassible.

Thomas responds with a gloss on 1 Corinthians 15:52 ("The dead will be raised imperishable, and we shall be changed") that asserts, "We — the good alone — will be changed with the unchangeableness and impassibility of glory." Thomas continues that as the body cooperates with the soul in life, so too will the glorified body share in the rewards or the punishments the soul has merited. Therefore, the bodies of the damned will suffer, which can occur only if their bodies are not rendered impassible. By divine justice, the fires of hell will not consume them, so that they may endure the everlasting punishment of experiencing the fire's pain without suffering destruction.

23

How All Will Know Our Sins and Our Merits

*Wherefore each man's conscience will be as a book
containing his deeds on which judgment will be
pronounced, even as in the human court
of law we make use of records.*

—ST, Supplement, 87, 1

*After the resurrection, will one know
all the sins one has committed?*

Several reasons have been offered to suggest that we will *not* recall
every sin we have committed when we face the Last Judgment.
These objections invoke, for instance, the limited capacity of the
human memory and the idea that memories of sin would cause
pain to the saints who rise in charity. It is through charity that
we grieve for our sins, and yet we read in Scripture that "He will
wipe away every tear from their eyes" (Rev. 21:4). Finally, some
argue that the damned will take solace in recalling their good
deeds, which will diminish their pain.

Thomas begins his response by recalling the words of Augustine, who said that "a kind of Divine energy will come to our aid,
so that we shall recall all of our sins to mind." Further, just as

human judgment is based upon external evidence, so too divine judgment is based on the witness of conscience: "Man looks on the outward appearance, but the LORD looks on the heart" (1 Sam. 16:7). Our conscience will bear witness to all our works, good and evil, so that they may be judged: "For we must all appear before the judgment seat of Christ, so that each one may receive good or evil, according to what he has done in the body" (2 Cor. 5:10). Further, "they show that what the law requires is written on their hearts, while their conscience also bears witness and their conflicting thoughts accuse or perhaps excuse them on that day when, according to my gospel, God judges the secrets of men by Christ Jesus" (Rom. 2:15–16). Each man's conscience will be like an open book, and as we read in Revelation 20:12: "I saw the dead, great and small, standing before the throne, and books were opened. Also another book was opened, which is the book of life. And the dead were judged by what was written in the books, by what they had done."

Thomas also replies that while charity produces guilt and grief over sin in this life, the saints in heaven will be so full of joy that they will have no room for sorrow. Instead of grieving over their past sins, they will rejoice in God's divine mercy, which forgave them for their sins. Further, by recalling their good deeds, the wicked will not diminish their pain, but will increase it, since they will remember all the good they have lost. As Boethius has said, "The greatest misfortune is to have been happy."

Will we be able to read everything that is in another person's conscience?

Of the various reasons for thinking that our sins will not be revealed to all people at the time of the Last Judgment, perhaps the most plausible is the argument that remembrance of sins, Confession, and penance blot out sin in this life. "But," St. John Chrysostom warns, "if thou forget [thy sins], thou wilt then remember them unwillingly, when they will be made public, and declared before all thy friends and foes, and in the presence of the holy angels." This would seem to indicate that only sins we have not confessed will be revealed to all.

Thomas begins by citing 1 Corinthians 4:5, which states that the Lord "will bring to light the things now hidden in darkness and will disclose the purposes of the heart." A gloss on this verse declares, "Deeds and thoughts both good and evil will then be revealed and made known to all." Thomas notes that while the past sins of all the saints will be blotted out, we can still come to know them, as we know the sins of saints such as Mary Magdalene, Peter, and David. When God comes as judge, He will know all the merits of the cases before Him, and like a jury, we will know them as well — not only our own sins and merits, but those of everyone else.

Thomas notes Lombard's opinion that sins blotted out by Confession would not be revealed, but Thomas believes it more probable that all sins and merits will be revealed; otherwise, we would not know perfectly the penance the saints did for their sins, "which would detract considerably from the glory of the saints and the praise due to God for having so mercifully delivered them." The revelation of the sins of the saints will not bring them disgrace; instead, they will be honored for their repentance, just as a confessor hails a person who confesses great crimes. To say that sins are blotted out means that "God sees them not for the purpose of punishing them."

*Will everyone's merits and demerits be
visible to all at a single glance?*

That we could see all of our sins and merits and those of others
instantaneously, "at a single glance," may seem hard to believe,
given the limitations of the human intellect. After all, Aristotle
has rightly observed that "we do not arrive at understanding
several things at the same time." So why should we think such
instantaneous knowledge will be possible? Well, Thomas starts
by citing Job 8:22: "Those who hate you will be clothed with
shame." A gloss on this verse declares, "As soon as they shall
see the Judge, all their evils deeds will stand before their eyes."
Augustine also notes that because an actual material book containing the deeds of all would be immeasurably enormous, and
an inconceivable amount of time would be necessary to consider
all merits and demerits individually, we must conclude that "each
one sees them all at the same time."

Thomas notes two opinions on the issue. Some say that
everyone will see his own merits and demerits and those of everyone else at the same time. While this far exceeds the natural
powers of the human intellect, it is credible in regard to the
blessed, because they will be able to see all things at once in
the Word Himself.

This would not apply to the damned, however, since their
intellect will not be raised to see God and all else in Him. So
some say that the wicked will see all their sins and those of others generally or "generically" at the same time, but will not see
each and every one down to its particulars at the same time. Still,
Augustine says that "they will count them all with one glance
of the mind," but "what is known generically is not counted."
Thomas suggests we choose a middle way: the damned will not

know each sin instantaneously, but in a very short time, through the assistance of divine power. This idea agrees with another saying of Augustine's that "they will be discerned with wondrous rapidity."[72]

---

[72] Perhaps you will recall that Thomas has described a similar phenomenon twice before, once in chapter 13 when describing the rapidity with which the angels will gather the matter for our bodies at the resurrection (*ST*, Supplement, 77, 4) and again in chapter 20 when describing the rapid movements made possible by the agility of our glorified bodies (*ST*, Supplement, 84, 3).

24

The Time and Place of the General Judgment

*Each man is both an individual person and a part of
the whole human race: wherefore a twofold judgment is
due to him. One, the particular judgment, is that
to which he will be subjected after death, when he will
receive according as he hath done in the body . . . not
indeed entirely but only in part since he will receive not
in the body but only in the soul. The other judgment
will be passed on him as a part of the human race.*

—ST, Supplement, 88, 1

Will there be a general judgment?

Some verses in Scripture seem to suggest that there will be no
general judgment at the time of the resurrection, since we all will
have received a particular judgment regarding our destination
after death. For example, we read in Nahum 1:9 that "He will
not take vengeance twice on his foes." Thomas counters with the
clear words of Matthew 12:41: "The men of Nineveh will arise
at the judgment with this generation and condemn it." Further,
per John 5:28–29, the time will come when "all who are in the
tombs will hear his voice and come forth, those who have done

good, to the resurrection of life, and those who have done evil, to the resurrection of judgment."

Thomas elaborates by describing God's "twofold operation." First, He *created* the world; gave things their being, their nature, and their distinct characteristics that contribute to the perfection of creation; and then rested (Gen. 2:2). Second, He *governs* creatures, as we read in John 5:17: "My Father is working still, and I am working." Governance requires judgment. Indeed, it requires a twofold judgment: each individual will be judged first according to his works and then "as adapted to the government of the universe." The Letter to the Hebrews tells us that one person's good is delayed for the benefit of others. Those who die in faith do not immediately receive all that was promised them, "since God had foreseen something better for us, that apart from us they should not be made perfect" (11:40). Here on earth, divine justice is not always made manifest, and we are not separated from the wicked, because there are opportunities for the good to profit or learn from the deeds of the wicked and for the wicked to profit from the good. At the Last Judgment, there will be no more time for such profit, and the wicked and the good will be completely separated for eternity.

In sum, Thomas provides the quotation that started this chapter. The *particular* judgment will assess each person as an *individual*, while the *general* judgment will assess us as *members of the human race*. The general judgment is not contrary to Nahum's prophecy that God will not take vengeance twice on His foes. God "will not inflict two punishments for one sin, and the punishment which before the judgment was not inflicted completely will be completed at the last judgment, after which the wicked will be tormented at the same time in body and soul."

Will the judgment take place through spoken words?

Thomas uses the phrase *per locutionem vocalem*—by spoken words —and notes that some believe the Last Judgment will indeed take place by audible word of mouth. Augustine declared that "it is uncertain how many days this judgment will last." Gregory wrote, "Those at least will hear the words of the Judge, who have confessed their faith in Him by words." Further, we know Christ will judge in His human form. This all suggests that the Last Judgment will not take place only in the mind (by the "inner word," as Thomas puts it) because it will take time; all will hear it; and just as Christ as man was visible to all, so will His words be audible to all.

Thomas begins his response with Augustine's claim that a "divine energy" will enable all to remember all their good or bad works "with wondrous rapidity ... so that all and each will be judged at the same moment." Should each merit of every person be discussed by word of mouth, all of us could not possibly be judged at the same moment. Further, we read in Romans 2:15–16 that people's consciences and thoughts will bear witness at the time of judgment. "Therefore," per Thomas, "seemingly, this sentence and the entire judgment will take place mentally." He elaborates that we cannot be certain of the answer to this question, though he finds it more probable that "the accusation of the wicked and the approval of the good or again as regards the sentence on both, will take place mentally," because if each individual were actually to express all his deeds by word of mouth, it "would require an inconceivable length of time." Christ will indeed appear bodily so that He will be suddenly visible to everyone, but speech requires time, and it "would require an immense length of time, if the judgment took place by word of mouth."

Can we know the time of the future judgment?

You may recall that in question 73 (covered in chapter 9 of this book), Thomas briefly addressed signs preceding the Last Judgment and concluded that we cannot know for sure when the judgment will take place, since Christ "will come like a thief in the night" (1 Thess. 5:2). Further, Christ told us, "But of that day or that hour no one knows, not even the angels in heaven, nor the Son, but only the Father" (Mark 13:32). Thomas elaborates that God causes things through His knowledge, and He bestows some knowledge and some secondary powers of causation on His creatures. Still, He reserves some knowledge and power to Himself and to no other creature. This applies foremost to things that are subject to His divine power alone, in which creatures do not cooperate with Him. Such will be the case with the end of the world: "For the world will come to an end by no created cause, even as it derived its existence immediately from God." Indeed, God Himself makes this clear: "It is not for you to know times or seasons which the Father has fixed by his own authority" (Acts 1:7).[73]

Will the judgment take place in the Valley of Josaphat?[74]

Joel 3:2 says, "I will gather all the nations and bring them down in the Valley of Jehoshaphat, and I will enter into judgment

---

[73] To adapt a colloquial phrase, we could say that such matters are literally "none of our business"!

[74] Spelled "Jehoshaphat" in the RSVCE. Since the time of Jerome in the fourth century A.D., Catholic tradition has typically identified it with the Cedron (or Kidron) Valley northeast of the Old City of Jerusalem.

with them there." Still, some think the judgment of mankind cannot possibly take place in that valley, because it is simply far too small a space.[75] Thomas makes clear that "we cannot know with any great certainty the manner in which this judgment will take place, nor how men will gather together to the place of judgment." Still, he cites Acts 1:11: "This Jesus, who was taken up from you into heaven, will come in the same way as you saw him go into heaven." Therefore, it seems probable that as Christ ascended near Mount Olivet, which is at the edge of the Valley of Josaphat, so He will return there as well "to show that He who descends is the same as He who ascended."

---

[75] The valley is about twenty miles long. Its depth and breadth vary, but are in the hundreds of feet.

25

Those Who Will Judge
and Those Who Will Be Judged

Wherefore those who will consent with Christ the Judge,
by approving His sentence, will be said to judge. . . . Wherefore
it is written (Wisdom 3:7–8): "The just . . . shall judge nations."

—ST, Supplement, 89, 1

Will humans judge together with Christ?

It may seem that no human beings will be involved in judging with Christ. According to John 5:22, 23, "the Father . . . has given all judgment to the Son, that all may honor the Son." Still, we read in Matthew 19:28, "You who have followed me will also sit on twelve thrones, judging the twelve tribes of Israel," and in Isaiah 3:14, "The Lord enters into judgment with the elders and princes of his people."

In reply, Thomas addresses several senses of the word "judgment," and then expounds upon Revelation 20:12, which refers to the judgment and the opening of the books that reveal what all have done. He draws on insights from Richard of St. Victor (1110–1173), who declared that those who read and contemplate the divine Word every day write its wisdom on their hearts, and "what else are the hearts of those who judge, divinely instructed in all truth, but a codex of the law?"

The proper action of judging, Thomas says, is exercised by the judge, who pronounces judgment and has dominion and authority over others. This sense of judgment belongs to God alone. Secondly, to judge can mean to make others aware of their sentence, delivered by another's authority, thereby leading them to the knowledge of divine justice. This is the kind of judgment in which humans will participate. The Son's judgment described in John 5 belongs to "the judgment of authority, which belongs to Christ alone."

Does judicial power correspond to voluntary poverty?

As we saw above, in Matthew 19:28, Jesus told the twelve apostles they would sit in twelve judgment seats. Some thought this meant they would be the only human judges. Thomas responds, "On the contrary, It is written (Job 36:6): 'He saveth not the wicked, and He giveth judgment to the poor.'"[76] Further, a gloss on Matthew 19:29 notes that Jesus' words applied not only to the twelve apostles, but also to all who give up everything they have to follow God. All "who made right use of what they had lawfully will be judged."

Thomas provides three reasons why voluntary poverty fittingly leads to the exercise of judicial power at the final judgment:

1. Voluntary poverty is embraced by "those who despise all the things of the world and cleave to Christ alone."

---

[76] The Latin Bible Thomas used employed the word *pauperum*, which translates to "the poor." The RSVCE uses "the afflicted."

Hence, they will judge justly, "as loving the truth of justice above all things."

2. Those who embrace voluntary poverty warrant exceptional merit because of their humility, which makes them contemptible in the eyes of the world. "He who humbles himself for Christ's sake shall be exalted" with judicial power.

3. Those who embrace poverty in order to follow Christ and contemplate divine truth are properly disposed to judging in accordance with divine truth, as Richard of St. Victor explained in the previous question.

As a further rebuttal to the notion that only the twelve apostles will assist in the judgment, Thomas cites Augustine, who stated that "the number twelve … signifies the whole multitude of those who will judge."

Will the angels judge?

Some believe the angels will judge for the following reasons: they will come with the Son of Man at the time of judgment (Matt. 25:31); one of the orders of angels is called "thrones," which pertains to judicial power; man will become equal to the angels (Matt. 22:30);[77] and we know that man will judge.

Thomas replies with the words of John 5:26–27: "The Father … has given [the Son] authority to execute judgment, because he is the Son of man." Thomas notes that the judgment of man requires that both the judge and his assessors (assistants in judging)

---

[77] This is the passage cited in the *Summa*. In the RSVCE, Matthew 22:30 says that after the resurrection, we will be "like angels," while Luke 20:36 explicitly states we will be "equal to angels."

share in human nature, which the angels do not. The angels will play a role as Christ's ministers at the judgment, according to Matthew 13:41: "The Son of man will send his angels, and they will gather out of his kingdom all causes of sin and all evildoers." A gloss indicates that the angels will not judge men, but will witness to men's deeds, "because it was under their guardianship that men did well or ill." Thomas notes that the thrones do execute and promulgate God's judgments, but as we noted, Christ must perform the Last Judgment, and with human assessors only. Men are promised an essential award equal with that of the angels—namely, the Beatific Vision—but this does not mean man cannot receive additional accidental (nonessential) rewards that the angels do not possess, "as in the case of the virgins' and martyrs' crowns: and the same may be said of the judicial power."[78]

*Will the demons execute
the judge's sentence on the damned?*

Opinions have differed on whether the demons will carry out the judge's sentence on the damned. Some argue, for example, that since the demons sinned more grievously than men, it would be unjust for men to be tortured by demons.

Thomas says we cannot know the answer with certainty, but since by sinning the damned have voluntarily subjected themselves to the devil, it would be just for them to be subjected to him in their punishments, "and punished by him as it were." Further, "just as the Divine illuminations are conveyed to men

[78] We will examine such additional "accidental" rewards in chapters 32 and 33.

by the good angels, so too the demons execute the Divine Justice on the wicked." Thomas notes as well that punishing the damned in hell will not bring joy to or lessen the pain of the demons, "since even in torturing others they are themselves tortured, because then the fellowship of the unhappy will not lessen but will increase unhappiness."[79]

Will all mankind be present at the judgment?

There are several reasons for thinking that not all will be present at the Last Judgment. Matthew 19:28, for example, refers to the twelve tribes of Israel, and not all people belong to those tribes. We read in Psalm 1:5 that "the wicked will not stand in the judgment." Further, at the judgment, human merits will be discussed, and children who die before the age of reason have acquired no merits.

Thomas responds to the contrary with Acts 10:42: "[Christ] is the one ordained by God to be judge of the living and the dead," that is, to be judge of everyone. Further, Revelation 1:7 says, "Behold, he is coming with the clouds, and every eye will see him." Thomas elaborates that since Christ shed His blood for all, it is fitting that all will be present at the judgment.

Responding to the objections, Thomas cites Augustine, who notes the twelve tribes of Israel stand for all other nations as well. The wicked will not arise to judge, but they will arise to be judged. As for children, they will arise at the Last Judgment "not to be judged, but to see the Judge's glory."

---

[79] Thomas notes that while we will not have a guardian angel after life on earth, each person in heaven "will have an angel to reign with him, in hell a demon to punish him" (*ST*, I, 133, 4).

Will the good be judged at the judgment?

In the first objection, we read that "it is declared (John 3:18) that 'he that believeth in Him is not judged.'[80] Now all the good believed in Him. Therefore they will not be judged." Thomas responds that all the good will be judged, for we read in 2 Corinthians 5:10: "For we must all appear before the judgment seat of Christ, so that each one may receive good or evil, according to what he has done in the body." He notes as well that the word "general" (*universale* in Latin) in "general judgment" includes everybody.

To address other objections, Thomas hones in on two key components of the general judgment—the discussion of merits and the payment of rewards. All will receive payment of rewards, even the good, according to their own merits. Those who have so completely renounced the things of the world and have so devoted themselves to divine service that they have "no notable admixture of evil merit," will be *saved*, but *not judged*. The faithful who have served God, but have not completely renounced sin and come to Him with the "wood, hay, straw" (1 Cor. 3:12) of venial sin, will be subjected to a discussion of their merits, "and yet they will be saved" (after their time in purgatory).

Will the wicked be judged?

Some think not all the wicked will be judged because "he who does not believe is condemned already" (John 3:18) and

---

[80] In Thomas's Latin Bible, the passage ends with *non iudicatur*, translated appropriately as "not judged." The RSVCE uses the word "condemned" instead of "judged." Thomas also happens to note in his reply to objection 1 that "judgment is sometimes used to express condemnation."

damnation is certain for those who die in mortal sin. Therefore, the wicked will not be judged. Thomas notes, however, that the wicked will be punished not only with damnation, but also "according to the degree of their guilt," which requires judgment. Unbelievers who reject God lack faith, and their deeds obtain no merit. Still, they will stand judged, for "without faith it is impossible to please [God]" (Heb. 11:6). Believers who die in mortal sin, but were "at least counted as citizens of the City of God will be judged as citizens," and their merits will be discussed before their sentence is passed. This discussion of their sins will also show to all present that they were "justly banished from the city of the saints, of which they appeared outwardly to be citizens."

Will the angels be judged?

It seems that men may judge angels, as we read in 1 Corinthians 6:3: "Do you not know that we are to judge angels?" Thomas notes, as we have seen previously, that God will not judge the same thing a second time (Nah. 1:9), and we read in John 16:11 that the prince of this world has already been judged. He elaborates that the good and the wicked angels were judged immediately at the time they chose to follow God or Satan. There is nothing more in them to be judged, since the good angels have no evil, and the evil angels have no good. Yet further retribution (reward to the good angels and punishment to the bad) will come to pass at the final judgment to the degree that the good angels will experience increased joy through the salvation of the souls they prompted toward meritorious deeds, and the bad angels will experience increased torment through the souls they helped lead to damnation. As for the text from 1 Corinthians, this does not mean humans will actually pronounce judgment on angels, but "refers to the judgment of comparison, because certain men will be found to be placed higher than the angels."

26

Here Comes the Judge! On the Form in Which He Will Appear to Us

Now Christ was judged by Pilate with regard to His human nature. Therefore He will judge under the human nature.

—ST, Supplement, 90, 1

Will Christ judge under the form of His humanity?

Some believe Christ will not come to judge in the form of His humanity because judgment requires authority and invincible power in the judge. Christ's authority over the living and the dead (Acts 10:42) and His invincible power come from not His humanity, but His Godhead. Others point to the following verses from John's Gospel: "The Father judges no one, but has given all judgment to the Son, that all may honor the Son, even as they honor the Father" (5:22–23). Christ's humanity is not the source of His equal honor with the Father, so He will not judge in human form.

Thomas begins his response by directing us to John 5:27, where we read that God the Father "has given [the Son] authority to execute judgment, because he is the Son of man." Christ has judicial authority not only because He created us, but also because He redeemed us through His death on the Cross in human form. By taking away the sins of humanity, Christ made it possible for man to enter heaven. Indeed, He redeemed and restored not only man, but also all creatures, as it is written: "For in him all the fulness of God was pleased to dwell, and through him to reconcile to himself all things, whether on earth or in heaven, making peace by the blood of his cross" (Col. 1:19–20), and "All authority in heaven and on earth has been given to me" (Matt. 28:18).

In response to the objections, Thomas states that Christ's divine nature gives Him "authority of lordship" over all creation, "but in respect of His human nature He has authority of lordship merited through His Passion." Further, Christ's human nature possesses invincible power that is not derived from natural human powers, but is "derived from His Godhead, whereby all things are subjected under His feet (1 Corinthians 15:25–28; Hebrews 2:8–9). Hence He will judge in His human *nature* indeed, but by the *power* of His Godhead" (italics added). He is equally honored with the Father and has obtained His judicial power because He is God — He could not have redeemed humanity as a mere man — "and consequently is to be honored equally with the Father, not as man but as God."

Will Christ judge in His glorified humanity?

Thomas presents a full five objections, based on flawed interpretations of Scripture and of passages from St. John Chrysostom and Augustine that seemingly claim Christ will appear in the scarred and wounded form of His crucified body, not in His glorified body.

Thomas first responds with the words of Luke 21:27: "And then they will see the Son of man coming in a cloud with power and great glory," meaning Christ will appear in His glorified body. Thomas notes that a judge should be more conspicuous than those who are judged. At the judgment, the blessed will appear in glorified bodies. "Much more therefore will the Judge appear in a glorified form." Further, at His first coming, when Christ came *to be judged*, He appeared in the form of weakness; therefore, at the Second Coming, when He comes *to judge*, "He will appear in the form of glory."[81]

Christ will appear in glory to manifest to all that He has come "by reason of His communication with the Father" and "to execute the Father's justice on men." Christ will appear in the same flesh, but in its glorified from. The scars on His body will not manifest weakness, but "the exceeding power whereby Christ overcame His enemies by His Passion and infirmity."

Will the wicked be able to see the Godhead without experiencing joy?

It seems to some that the wicked will be able to see the Godhead without experiencing joy, for they will know with certainty that Christ is God at the Second Coming, and yet, while seeing His Godhead, they will not rejoice. "Therefore it will be possible to see it without joy."

Thomas responds, to the contrary, "This is eternal life, that they know thee the only true God, and Jesus Christ whom thou hast sent" (John 17:3). Clearly, then, "the essence of bliss consists in seeing God. Now joy is essential to bliss. Therefore the Godhead cannot be seen without joy." The essence of the Godhead

---

[81] See also CCC 681: "On Judgment Day at the end of the world, Christ will come in glory."

is the essence of truth. This is delightful to everyone by nature, since, as Aristotle noted, we "all naturally desire to know." Therefore, one cannot see the Godhead without experiencing joy. Those who are damned will indeed know that Christ is God, but *only through the manifest signs of His Godhead* when He returns. They will not receive the reward of seeing His Godhead, since no one can see it and not experience joy, for God in His essence is goodness itself, as well as truth.

27

The Nature of the Universe after Judgment Day

*This disposition of newness will be neither natural
nor contrary to nature, but above nature (just as
grace and glory are above the nature of the soul):
and it will proceed from an everlasting agent
which will preserve it for ever.*

—*ST*, Supplement, 91, 1

Will the earth be renewed?

For a variety of reasons, based on Scripture and philosophy, some believe the world will not be made anew at the Last Judgment. It is written, for example, that "what has been is what will be ... and there is nothing new under the sun" (Eccles. 1:9). Also, the philosopher Empedocles (495–435 B.C.) and the theologian Origen argued that any change in creation would be unnatural, and according to Aristotle, what is unnatural and accidental cannot last forever. Therefore, the new world would eventually pass away and return in an endless cycle of recurrence.

Thomas counters with the words of Isaiah 65:17: "Behold, I create new heavens and a new earth; and the former things shall not be remembered or come into mind." He also cites

Revelation 21:1: "Then I saw a new heaven and a new earth; for the first heaven and the first earth had passed away." Thomas notes as well that as "every creature loves its like" (Sir. 13:15), man has some likeness to the universe and is sometimes called "a little world." Humans love the universe naturally and desire its good. Therefore, to satisfy our desire, God will make the universe better.

Indeed, God made all corporeal things for humanity's sake, and they serve us in two ways. First, they sustain our bodily life, and secondly, we come to know God through them. As we read in Romans 1:20, "Ever since the creation of the world his invisible nature, namely, his eternal power and deity, has been clearly perceived in the things that have been made."[82]

Now, after the resurrection, we will need the world neither for bodily sustenance (since our glorified bodies will be incorruptible) nor to lead our souls to God, since we will see God in His essence. Still, we will not see Him with our corporeal, physical eyes, even in our glorified state, but through intellectual knowledge. Nonetheless, our corporeal eyes will delight in seeing "the Godhead in Its corporeal effects, wherein manifest proofs of the Divine majesty will appear, especially in Christ's flesh,

---

[82] Indeed, this passage is a cornerstone of Thomas's famous five arguments that demonstrate the existence of God and explain His fundamental attributes, such as perfection, infiniteness, goodness, and so on. It is valid to reason *a posteriori*, that is, to reason from things already known to us to things not yet known. We can see and know the effects of God and then reason from them that His existence is their cause. If an effect exists, we know that its cause must have preceded it. This is why, in 1870, the First Vatican Council declared dogmatically that certain knowledge of God can be attained through "the natural light of human reason" (quoted in CCC 36).

and secondarily in the bodies of the blessed, and afterwards in all other bodies," which will receive from God "a greater inflow from the Divine goodness than now."

Qoheleth's statement that "there is nothing new under the sun" is true for the natural course of the world, but it does not apply to the glorified universe, which will not be "under the sun." Further, in response to Empedocles and Origen, Thomas says the disposition of the new world will be "neither natural nor contrary to nature, but above nature (just as grace and glory are above the nature of the soul): and it will proceed from an everlasting agent which will preserve it for ever."

Will the heavenly bodies stop moving?

There are a variety of reasons to think that the resurrection will not alter the movement of heavenly bodies. Indeed, Thomas provides a full ten objections and lays out "three opinions touching this question" in his response. The fourth objection, for example, holds that the whole world will be improved when it is renewed. Movement contributes to the perfection of heavenly bodies, as they "participate in the divine goodness by their movement," according to Aristotle. Therefore, they will continue to move.

In a celestial nutshell, Thomas concludes that normal movement of heavenly bodies will cease. As we read in Isaiah 60:20, "Your sun shall no more go down, nor your moon withdraw itself; for the LORD will be your everlasting light." Further, Aristotle has shown that "the movement of the heaven is for the sake of continual generation in this lower world." The movement of celestial bodies influences things such as the temperature of our climate in accordance with the needs of plant, animal, and human life. Since all movement is for some end, all movement stops when this end is attained. After the resurrection, no more humans will be born, and we will not need the heavenly bodies to sustain life. This also provides the answer to the fourth objection, since movement contributes to the perfection of the heavenly bodies only when they cause generation and corruption in the lower world. When generation and corruption have ceased, so will the movement of heavenly bodies, without any loss of perfection.

Will the heavenly bodies grow brighter?

Some think the heavenly bodies will not grow brighter. For example, the lower bodies will be cleansed by fire, but that fire will not reach the heavenly bodies. Thomas responds with the clear words of Isaiah 30:26: "Moreover the light of the moon will be as the light of the sun, and the light of the sun will be sevenfold." The entire universe, including both the lower and the heavenly bodies, will be improved. This betterment will include enhancing their beauty. We read in Wisdom 13:5 that "from the greatness and beauty of created things comes a corresponding perception of their Creator." Further, the beauty of the heavenly bodies consists chiefly in their light: "The glory of the stars is the beauty of heaven, a gleaming array in the heights of the Lord" (Sir. 43:9). It remains to the delight of the blessed to see to what degree their beauty is enhanced, allowing them to reflect more intensely than ever the beauty and greatness of the God who created them.

As for the cleansing fire, it will serve to remove imperfections and sins from the lower bodies. The heavenly bodies do not share these imperfections. Their perfection will come not from fire, but from God's divine power, which will renew all things heavenly and otherwise.

Will the elements themselves become brighter?

Some argue that the elements and the lower bodies will not grow brighter, because the universe is perfected by its order and harmony, wherein the heavenly bodies possess brightness and the lower bodies do not. If brightness were given to lower, elemental bodies, this harmony would be destroyed.

Thomas responds first with the words of Revelation 21:1: "Then I saw a new heaven and a new earth." Both the heavens and the earth will be renewed. We have seen that our glorified bodies will receive brightness and clarity, which means that their elemental particles will also become bright. (We can literally say of the blessed that their future looks very bright!) When the universe is renewed, Thomas tells us, "the lower spirits will receive the properties of the higher spirits, because men will be as the angels in heaven," as Matthew 22:30 says. In like manner, since, per Aristotle, the lower bodies differ from the heavenly bodies chiefly in terms of their light and transparency, the lower bodies will be perfected chiefly in terms of their brightness. We should recall, too, that the world's renewal will come about so that man, even through his senses, may see the Godhead manifest in signs. Vision is the most noble and spiritual of our senses, and its power and pleasure will be increased by the enhancement of light in lower elemental and heavenly bodies.

As for the order and harmony of the universe, this will not be impaired by the betterment of the elements, "because all the other parts will also be bettered, and so the same harmony will remain."

28

Last Thoughts on the Last Things: Judgment

*When he comes at the end of time to judge the living and
the dead, the glorious Christ will reveal the secret disposition
of hearts and will render to each man according to his works,
and according to his acceptance or refusal of grace.*

—CCC 682

Thomas's treatment of the Last Judgment has certainly given us a great deal to ponder! Thomas addressed a total of nineteen questions, comprised of eighty-two articles. He started with question 73, "Of the Signs That Will Precede the Judgment" and ended with question 91, "Of the Quality of the World after the Judgment," taking up ninety-five pages of double-column print in the Supplement to the *Summa Theologica*. In this book, we condensed and summarized his arguments in nineteen chapters, comprised of eighty-two questions and answers, starting with chapter 9, "Signs That Will Precede the Last Judgment" and ending with chapter 27, "The Nature of the Universe after Judgment Day."

Our current *Catechism* addresses some of the dozens of issues Thomas discussed in this section of the *Summa*. I have tried to highlight this by citations in either the text or the footnotes, but I would also like to direct readers interested in reading more to particular sections in the *Catechism* most directly relevant to issues including Christ's Resurrection and our own, the Last Judgment, and the state of our bodies and the universe after the last Judgment. This material is found in paragraphs 638–682, which explicate the following statements of the Creed: "On the third day he rose again," "He ascended into heaven and is seated at the right hand of the Father," and "From thence he will come again to judge the living and the dead." Further, paragraphs 1020–1065 explicate the final line of the Creed: "I believe in life everlasting. Amen."

In part 2 of this book, we also examined many issues that are not clearly defined. On these points, like the great theologians before him, Thomas could only speculate and suggest probable answers. As St. Paul told us, we see through a "mirror dimly" here on earth, but should we rise to heaven, we will see God "face to face" (1 Cor. 13:12). Only then, through the Godhead we behold in the Beatific Vision, will we understand these mysterious realities.

I can only imagine which issues caught your attention and captured your imagination as we discussed Thomas's thoughts on the Last Judgment. Here, I would like to offer but a few last thoughts of my own.

Some readers may have noticed the absence of the so-called Rapture, wherein Christ instantaneously removes the elect alone from the earth before the final tribulation. An in-depth treatment of the Rapture is beyond the scope of this book, but I will note that this idea builds upon the chiliasm or millennialism Thomas debunked, as we first saw in chapter 13, "When and How All Will Arise."[83] While the millennialist heresy was alive and (un)well

---

[83] We also read in CCC 676 that the Church rejects millennialism.

in Thomas's day, the idea of a rapture before or during a literal millennium of tribulation on earth was not promulgated widely until the rise of Fundamentalism in the nineteenth century.[84]

As for issues that *were* addressed in the *Summa*, I found the discussion of who will carry out the judgment (examined in chapter 25 of this book) particularly interesting. I recall reading that certain saints have been said to assist Christ at Judgment Day—for example, St. Patrick is said to have asked to judge the Irish. Further, a decade or so ago, I was researching my namesake, St. Kevin of Glendalough, Ireland. I discovered an ancient Latin life of the saint, which told of his bargain with an angel who was coaxing him away from his life as a hermit in a beautiful wooded glen with two lakes (hence the name Glendalough). The angel asked him to come out of the woods and found a great monastery and churches. In the name of Christ, St. Kevin requested boons for his monastery and its tributaries, successors, and all its churches. As the legend goes, the angel agreed to all this. In addition, "the angel gave to him seven times the full of the glen in the Day of Judgement, and a little spear of red gold" to hold in his hand.[85] Now, with Thomas's help, we can see all the more clearly how the saints will indeed be rewarded with the honor of assisting Christ on Judgment Day.

I'll conclude with just one more thought that struck me as I read the writings of Thomas and the great Church Fathers and Doctors on these awe-inspiring topics. It seems to me that

---

[84] If you would like to take a closer look at this topic, see "The Rapture," Catholic Answers, accessed October 19, 2020, https://www.catholic.com/tract/the-rapture.

[85] "Life of Coemgen I," in Charles Plummer, *Lives of Irish Saints*, vol. 2 (New York: Oxford University Press, 1997), 124. Plummer uses the original Irish form of the name Kevin.

today's secular thinkers tend to focus only on the material world (what Thomas would call the "corporeal" realm) and dismiss even the possibility of the invisible, immaterial, and spiritual. This ideological stance, which many people assume is necessitated by modern science, is referred to as "materialism" or "physicalism."

Informed Catholics reject this erroneous, incomplete view of reality, but others who are poorly catechized may be at risk of embracing a slightly different error regarding our future life in eternity—namely, the rejection of not the spiritual realm, but the material or physical world. This error gives rise to a view of the afterlife that borders on Gnosticism, which rejects the goodness of the body.

Please allow me to explain. In his biography of St. Thomas, G. K. Chesterton wrote that as one saint bears the name "St. John of the Cross" (1542–1591), "the man we study may specially be called St. Thomas of the Creator."[86] A central theme appearing throughout Thomas's works is the inherent goodness of all creation, which is proclaimed again and again in the book of Genesis. Unlike the Gnostics and Manicheans, Thomas argues that this goodness is not exclusive to the spiritual realm, but most certainly extends to physical creation. The universe as a whole is good, and so is everything in it, including man in both body and soul.

Some modern theological perspectives run the risk of downplaying the reality and goodness of physical creation by portraying the afterlife as a purely spiritual "state" (as in a state of mind) and not an external reality. Of course, some ancient thinkers, most notably Plato, held similar views, thinking the soul alone would

---

[86] G. K. Chesterton, *Saint Thomas Aquinas: "The Dumb Ox"* (New York: Image Books, 1956), 119.

survive. Those who understand eternal life in this way may be shocked by Thomas's belief in the physical realities of heaven; purgatory; limbo; hell; and the glorious, impassible, subtle, agile, and luminously clarified *bodies* to which the souls of the blessed will be eternally united. Perhaps just as shocking for these quasi-Gnostics, Thomas builds on insights from Scripture to show how God will renew and perfect the physical universe and its elements for eternity.

These are hopefully intriguing insights to ponder, but rest assured, we have not yet heard Thomas's last words on the Four Last Things. We will now consider the *spiritual* and *physical* realities of the most important and lasting of the Four Last Things, one of unspeakable bliss and the other of a sad, but freely chosen misery.

Part 3

To Heaven for Those Who Accept It

In the next place we must consider matters concerning the blessed after the general judgment. We shall consider: (1) Their vision of the Divine essence, wherein their bliss consists chiefly; (2) Their bliss and their mansions; (3) Their relations with the damned; (4) Their gifts, which are contained in their bliss; (5) The crowns which perfect and adorn their happiness.

—ST, Supplement, 92, Prologue

29

On the Beatific Vision Bestowed on the Blessed

Even as we hold by faith that the last end of
man's life is to see God, so the philosophers maintained
that man's ultimate happiness is to understand
immaterial substances according to their being.

—ST, Supplement, 92, 1

Will the glorified human intellect
be able to see God in His essence?

This question has proven quite taxing to the not-yet-glorified intellects of many of God's brightest and most devout theologians over the centuries. Thomas provides a full *sixteen* objections (the most of any article in his "Treatise on the Resurrection") to the idea that the blessed will see God in His essence. There are indeed many reasons to think that the saints in heaven, and even the highest of angels, can never attain the capacity to see "I am" (Exod. 3:14) as He truly is.

Even the first objection on its own seems formidable. John 1:18 tells us that "no one has ever seen God," and St. John Chrysostom commented that "not even the heavenly essences, namely the Cherubim and Seraphim, have ever been able to see Him as He is." We are promised equality with the angels, since we read in Matthew 22:30 that those in heaven "are like the angels," indeed, "equal to angels" (Luke 20:36). If the angels cannot see God in His essence, then neither can the saints.

Other objections get *very* philosophically and theologically nuanced. I'll highlight the bottom lines of just a few: Dionysius wrote that knowledge pertains to existing things, which are finite. Since God is infinite and above all things, He is above all knowledge, and we can never know Him. Further, Dionysius wrote that "God is invisible on account of His surpassing glory." Now, since God's glory surpasses the human intellect "on the way" (here on earth), it will surpass our glorified intellects in heaven; furthermore, as He is invisible on the way, so too will He be invisible in heaven.

Thomas begins his response to the objections with a veritable barrage of scriptural passages, including the following:
- "For now we see in a mirror dimly, but then face to face" (1 Cor. 13:12). To see something face-to-face is to see it in its essence. "Therefore," Thomas says, "God will be seen in His essence by the saints in heaven."
- "When he appears we shall be like him, for we shall see him as he is" (1 John 3:2).
- "He who loves me will be loved by my Father, and I will love him and manifest myself to him" (John 14:21).

Thomas elaborates that the desire of the saints cannot be frustrated, and it is the common desire of all the saints to see God in His essence, as Scripture repeatedly reveals:
- "Show me Thy glory" (Exod. 33:13).[87]

---

[87] This is from the translation Thomas used in the *Summa*. In Latin, the passage ends with the words *gloriam tuam* (your glory). The RSVCE has "Show me now thy ways."

• "Show Thy face and we shall be saved" (Ps. 80 [79]:19).[88]
• "Show us the Father and it is enough for us" (John 14:8).[89]

Thomas then elaborates with the quotation that opened this chapter. We hold by faith that our last end, our highest good, our complete fulfillment and happiness, consists precisely in seeing God. Our intellects will indeed attain the divine vision in heaven. "It remains, then, to examine how this may come about." The examination that follows is truly fascinating, but might appear to some readers as abstract, abstruse, and unfamiliar as the two thinkers whom Thomas first cites: Alfarabius and Avempace.[90] Readers who care (and dare) to dip into Thomas's rich and detailed analyses may read question 92 of the Supplement. Here, I will keep things quite simple and summarize just a few of Thomas's answers to just a few of the objections.

First, Thomas addresses the scriptural passages stating that no one has seen God, including, according to St. John Chrysostom, the angels. From Augustine, Thomas borrows three ways of explaining these words: (1) no one sees God with corporeal vision (that is, with the eyes, as opposed to intellectual vision), (2) the intellectual vision of God is excluded from those who still dwell in mortal flesh, or (3) "the vision of comprehension" is excluded from any created intellect.

[88] This is verse 20 in Thomas's translation, which uses the words *ostende faciem tuam* (show thy face). The RSVCE has "Let thy face shine."
[89] The RSVCE translation is virtually identical: "Show us the Father, and we shall be satisfied."
[90] Alfarabius, or al-Farabi (872–950), was a renowned Muslim philosopher, as was Avempace, or Ibn Bajjah (1085–1138). And speaking of Muslim philosophers, Thomas also mentions Avicenna, or Ibn Sina (980–1037), in his response to one of the objections.

Thomas believes that St. John Chrysostom refers to this third sense, since his commentary on John 1:18 says, "By seeing, the evangelist means a most clear perception, and such a comprehension as the Father has of the Son." Thomas agrees that this is precisely what St. John the Evangelist meant, since he ended the same verse with the words "The only-begotten Son, who is in the bosom of the Father, he has made him known." Thomas says John intends "to prove the Son to be God from His comprehending God." In other words, those in heaven will, like the angels, see God face-to-face in His essence, but we will never fully grasp or comprehend Him as the Son does.

As for the objection that a finite intellect (even a glorified one) can never know an infinite object (God), Thomas replies that the vision whereby we will see God in His essence is, through God's gift, "the same whereby God sees Himself, as regards that whereby He is seen, because as He sees Himself in His essence so shall we also see Him." But a person can see more or less clearly depending on the power of his intellect, just as he can see an object, such as a simple stone, more or less clearly depending on his power of sight. Because our intellect is less powerful than God's, "consequently in that vision we shall see the same thing that God sees, namely His essence, but not so effectively."

As for God's glory, "it does not surpass the Divine essence, which will be the form of our intellect in heaven: and therefore although it is invisible now, it will be visible then." In other words, it will not exceed the capacity of our intellect.

Will the saints see God with the eyes of the glorified body?
Job 42:5 says, "I had heard of thee by the hearing of the ear, but now my eye sees thee." Further, Augustine said of our glorified

eyes, "A greater power will be in those eyes, not to see more keenly, as certain serpents or eagles are reported to see (for whatever acuteness of vision is possessed by these animals they can see only corporeal things), but to see even incorporeal things." This seems to suggest that our power of vision will be so perfected that our glorified eyes will be able to see God.

Thomas responds to the contrary, however, with multiple insights from the Church Fathers Ambrose, Jerome, and Augustine himself. Commenting on Luke 1:11 (in which the angel Gabriel appears to Zechariah), Ambrose declared, "God is not sought with the eyes of the body, nor surveyed by the sight, nor clasped by the touch." (After all, angels are spiritual beings, not corporeal ones.) Commenting on Isaiah 6:1, in which the prophet describes seeing God sitting upon His throne, Jerome says, "The Godhead not only of the Father, but also of the Son and of the Holy Ghost is visible, not to carnal eyes, but only to the eyes of the mind, of which it is said: Blessed are the pure in heart," for they shall see God (Matt. 5:8). Augustine said, "Man is said to be made in God's image inasmuch as he is able to see God." Thomas notes that "man is in God's image as regards his mind, and not as regards his flesh. Therefore he will see God with his mind and not with his flesh."

Thomas says we will not see God directly, even through the powers of our glorified eyes, though we will see Him through the powers of our intellect.[91] This is not to say that our glorified eyes

---

[91] If I might add a comment here: haven't we all said to someone, at some time, "Now I *see* what you are saying"? Of course, we do not literally *see* the spoken words of another person, but when we make such a statement, we do indeed say something very meaningful—that we have *grasped* (to use another bodily metaphor) or *understood* (that is, "to stand under"—yet another

will not add to our happiness and our union with God in heaven in other ways. Thomas says with sublime insight that

> on the one hand, the bodily sight will see so great a glory of God in bodies, especially in the glorified bodies and most of all in the body of Christ, and, on the other hand, the intellect will see God so clearly, that God will be perceived in things seen with the eye of the body, even as life is perceived in speech. For although our intellect will not then see God from seeing His creatures, yet it will see God in His creatures seen corporeally.

Indeed, in this way, our beatitude, which is chiefly of the soul, "passes from the soul on to the body by a kind of overflow."

In response to the objections, Thomas says the passage in Job refers to the spiritual eye, which St. Paul describes as "the eyes of your hearts enlightened" (Eph. 1:18). To clarify his comments on our glorified eyes, Augustine noted that we will see God according to "a greater power."

When the saints see God, will they see all that He sees?

This is another rather abstract and nuanced issue, prefaced by a full dozen philosophical and theological objections that by seeing God, our souls *will* see all the things God sees. To provide but one of the more straightforward objections, we read in Proverbs 10:24 that "the desire of the righteous will be granted." Since,

metaphor) the essence or meaning of what that person is saying. So, too, will our Beatific Vision of God's essence be profoundly meaningful, indeed the most profoundly meaningful experience of all.

per Aristotle, "all men desire naturally to know," and nature is not destroyed by glory, God will grant the saints' desire to know all things.

Thomas begins with insights from Dionysius, who noted that "the higher angels cleanse the lower angels from ignorance." The lower angels do see the divine essence, and yet they do not know all things on their own. The glorified human soul will not see God more perfectly than the angels do, so "the souls seeing God will not necessarily see all things." Of all who have shared in humanity, Christ alone has the fullness of the Spirit (John 3:34) and knows all things, for the Father "has given all things into his hand" (John 3:35).

As for the desire of the saints to know all things, it "will be fulfilled by the mere fact of their seeing God: just as their desire to possess all good things will be fulfilled by possessing God." As John 14:8 says, "Lord, show us the Father, and we shall be satisfied."

30

Happy Saints in Their Heavenly Mansions

It is manifest that the happiness of the saints
will increase in extent after the resurrection,
because their happiness will then be not only
in the soul but also in the body.

—*ST*, Supplement, 93, 1

Will the saints be happier after
the judgment than they were before?

One reason some think the saints in heaven will not be happier after the Last Judgment than they already are is that the nearer something is to God's divine likeness, the more it participates in His happiness. The saints now exist as purely spiritual souls, so their happiness is actually greater than it will be when they are reunited with their bodies.

Thomas responds with a gloss on the verse "I saw under the altar the souls of those who had been slain for the word of God" (Rev. 6:9). According to the gloss, "at the present the souls of the saints are under the altar"; that is, they are "less exalted than they will be." Therefore, the happiness of the saints will increase after the resurrection.

Thomas elaborates with the wonderful statement that opened this chapter, and he adds that the soul will rejoice not only in its own good, but also in the good of the body. The happiness of the saints will come to fill not only their souls, but also their glorified bodies. What a thing to imagine! God made man as a composite being of body and soul, and after the resurrection, man's soul will be reunited with the glorified body, making all the blessed whole again in unequalled perfection and happiness. When body and soul are reunited and glorified, the blessed will be more like God and in greater union with Him, because they will be more perfect in their being. The more perfect a thing is, the more it is like God.

Should the degrees of beatitude be called mansions?

Christ told us that there are many mansions in His Father's house (John 14:2).[92] Some say we should be very cautious about interpreting this to mean that there will be different degrees of happiness (beatitude) in heaven. Beatitude implies the notion of a reward, while mansions do not. Further, mansions imply different *physical* places in which bodies reside. The place where the saints will be beatified is *spiritual*, and there is just one such place, "namely God Who is one."

Thomas responds that Augustine has explained that *Christ did indeed mean there are different degrees of rewards in heaven.* Thomas then notes that the heavenly kingdom is compared to

---

[92] The RSVCE uses the word "rooms" instead of mansions. In the *Summa* and the Latin Bible Thomas used, the word is *mansiones*. Neither translation alters the meaning of this question or Thomas's answer.

a city in Revelation 21:2. Just as a well-ordered city has different mansions, so too will heaven be comprised of multiple mansions "according to the various degrees of beatitude." All the blessed will experience beatitude, though some to a higher degree than others. Aristotle explained that every resting place of a thing in motion is an establishment or mansion (*collocatio* in Latin). The end of the movements of the appetites and will consists in the happiness of beatitude, when what was sought has been attained in heaven.

Even in heaven, there will be different degrees of beatitude. Different saints will reside in different "mansions" that vary in their closeness to God. To give a comparison from nature, lighter objects (balloons, let's say) will rise higher than heavier objects. The lighter the balloon, the higher it will rise and rest.

Are the mansions distinguished according to degrees of charity?

So what causes some saints to rise higher than others? Some think this is due to our natural powers, for the Master gives "to each according to his ability" (Matt. 25:15). Others think it is due to our works, for it is written: "Thou dost requite a man according to his work" (Ps. 62 [61]:12).

Thomas notes, to the contrary, that neither our natural abilities nor the works produced by our own efforts will determine our place and happiness in heaven. Rather, "the more one will be united to God the happier will one be. Now the measure of charity is the measure of one's union with God. Therefore the diversity of beatitude will be according to the difference of charity." The possibility for beatitude in heaven derives from charity, that theological, God-infused virtue that unites us to Him.

Further, the more charity one has, the higher one's beatitude will be. Those with the highest degree of charity will experience the Beatific Vision with the greatest clarity.

Good works are important, but works alone do not yield spiritual merit unless they are inspired by charity. (After all, one can do good deeds for reasons other than love of God and neighbor, such as the desire for fame or some future personal gain.) Those who possess and share the greatest love will enjoy the highest "mansions."

As for the reference to ability in Matthew 25:15, this denotes "not the natural ability alone, but the natural ability together with the endeavor to obtain grace." This natural ability perfected by grace will dispose one to higher degrees of charity, and it is the degree of charity attained, and not natural ability alone, that will determine one's degree of beatitude in heaven.

31

How the Saints Relate to the Damned

*Charity is the principle of pity when it is possible for
us out of charity to wish the cessation of a person's
unhappiness. But the saints cannot desire this for the
damned, since it would be contrary to Divine justice.*

—ST, Supplement, 94, 2

*Will the saints in heaven see
the sufferings of the damned?*

The prophet Isaiah reports that the people of God cried out,
"Look down from heaven and see.... For thou art our Father,
though Abraham does not know us and Israel does not acknowledge us" (63:15, 16). A gloss from Augustine on this verse says,
"The dead, even the saints, know not what the living, even their
own children, are doing." Some argue that "much less therefore"
do the saints in heaven see the sufferings of the damned.

Thomas begins his response by citing another verse from Isaiah: "They shall go forth and look on the dead bodies of the men
that have rebelled against me" (66:24). A gloss adds, "The elect
will go out by understanding or seeing manifestly, so that they
may be urged the more to praise God." Thomas elaborates that

everything is known better when it is compared to its contrary, because when contrary things are seen together, the differences become more conspicuous. The saints will indeed see the suffering of the damned. It will not decrease their happiness, but will actually increase it, in a way, for the punishment of the damned will display God's divine justice.

The first passage from Isaiah speaks of the saints' inability to know by natural knowledge what happens to the living. As Gregory has pointed out, however, the saints in heaven, possessing "the glory of God within them," will indeed be granted the power to know all that happens to "wayfarers" on earth and to the damned.

Will the saints in heaven pity the unhappiness of the damned?

One might think that the blessed in heaven will pity the damned. Pity flows from charity, and charity is most perfect among the saints in heaven. Thomas notes, though, that whoever pities another shares to some degree in that person's unhappiness. The saints will be completely happy; therefore, they will not pity the damned. Thomas explains that mercy, compassion, or pity may arise in people in two ways: either through passion or by reasoned choice. The saints, being impassible, will experience no passions in their lower powers that do not result from reasoned choice. We pity another person rationally when we wish his evil to be dispelled, but the saints will not wish the evil experienced by the damned to be dispelled, because it is in accord with divine justice. Therefore, *pity born of charity is given to sinners on earth* by the just, the angels, and God, because there is still hope for their salvation.

Will the saints rejoice in the punishment of the wicked?

Some argue that to rejoice in another's evil is hateful. The saints in heaven will have no hatred, and they will not rejoice in the punishment of the damned. Further, the saints will have attained the greatest possible conformity to God, and just as God does not rejoice in our afflictions, so too will the blessed not rejoice in the afflictions of the damned.

Thomas points out, to the contrary, that "the righteous will rejoice when he sees the vengeance" (Ps. 58 [57]:10). Now, the saints will not rejoice directly in the punishment of the wicked, but they will rejoice indirectly insofar as the punishment of the damned is in accord with divine justice. The saints will also rejoice that they have been delivered from punishment. Therefore, "Divine justice and their own deliverance will be the direct cause of the joy of the blessed: while the punishment of the damned will cause it indirectly."

Rejoicing directly in another's suffering is hateful, but it is not hateful to rejoice in something else related to that suffering. Indeed, here on earth, we are to rejoice even in our own afflictions and sufferings when we see that they help us merit eternal life: "Count it all joy, my brethren, when you meet various trials" (James 1:2).

32

Additional Gifts for the Blessed

Without doubt the blessed when they are brought into glory
are dowered by God with certain gifts for their adornment,
and this adornment is called their dowry by the masters.

—*ST*, Supplement, 95, 1

Should the gifts of the blessed
be called their "dowry"?

As we see in our opening quotation, theologians speak of special
gifts of adornment God gives to the blessed in heaven. They
called these gifts the "dowry" of the saints. Some think this term
is inappropriate for several reasons, which Thomas lists in five
objections. To give a few examples, the first objection holds that
a dowry is given to a bridegroom to provide for the needs of the
marriage. The saints in heaven resemble not the bridegroom,
but the bride. Further, a dowry pertains to external, physical
goods, while the reward of the blessed will consist of internal,
spiritual goods.

Thomas begins his discussion with a verse from Scripture
wherein St. Paul, after referencing the union of husband and
wife in marriage, says, "This is a great mystery, and I mean in

reference to Christ and the Church" (Eph. 5:32). Earthly marriage signifies the spiritual, heavenly marriage to come. Just as an earthly dowered bride is brought to dwell in the house of the groom, so too the saints will be brought to Christ's dwelling and "dowered by God with certain gifts." Further, earthly dowry is given to ease the marriage. "But the spiritual marriage is more blissful than the carnal marriage. Therefore a dowry should be especially assigned thereto." Also, the dowry serves to adorn the bride, and the saints are adorned when they are "taken into glory," according to Isaiah 61:10: "He has clothed me with the garments of salvation … as a bride adorns herself with her jewels." There is no doubt, Thomas says, that the glorified blessed will be adorned with additional gifts by God and given the dowry that "is the everlasting adornment of soul and body adequate to life, lasting for ever in eternal bliss."

As for the first objection, while a dowry is generally given to the bridegroom for his use, the bride retains control and ownership of it "by the fact that if the marriage be dissolved, the dowry reverts to the bride according to law." Accordingly, in spiritual marriage, the adornments that God bestows on the bride (the saints of the Church) do belong to Him in the sense that they contribute to His honor and glory, yet they belong to the saints as their adornment. While external, physical goods contribute to the "outward comeliness" of the bride, spiritual marriage requires "inward comeliness," according to the Psalms: "All the glory of the king's daughter is within" (45 [44]:14).[93] The dowry increases the inward comeliness of the blessed.

---

[93] Thomas's Latin Bible. The RSVCE has "The daughter of the king is decked in her chamber with gold-woven robes" (v. 13).

Is the dowry the same as beatitude?

It might seem that the dowry is the same as beatitude, since, for example, Boethius has written that "'beatitude is a state made perfect by the aggregate of all good things.' Now the state of the blessed is perfected by the dowries. Therefore the dowries are part of beatitude."

Thomas responds to the contrary that dowries are given freely without merit, "whereas beatitude is not given, but is awarded in return for merits. Therefore beatitude is not a dowry."

Thomas elaborates that beatitude is *one* thing, and there are *several* dowries; furthermore, beatitude is within a person's *soul*, which, as Aristotle notes, is principal to man. Yet the dowries are given to the glorified *body*. Thomas concludes that beatitude and the dowries are different things because beatitude is "the perfect operation itself by which the soul is united with God, while the dowries are habits or dispositions or any other qualities directed to this same perfect operation, so that they are directed to beatitude," but are not parts of beatitude itself. This also addresses the objection based on Boethius's definition of "beatitude." Beatitude is the sum total of all goods not in the sense that all these goods (such as the dowries) are essential parts of beatitude, but because they assist or are directed to beatitude.

Should Christ receive a dowry?

Some think Christ will receive a dowry, because a dowry is due to all members of the Church, since the Church is the heavenly bride. According to 1 Corinthians 12:27, Christ is a member of the Church: "Now you [the Church] are the body of Christ and individually members of it," that is, of Christ, according to a gloss. Therefore, a dowry is also due to Christ.

The fifth objection Thomas presents is interesting because it gives us the names of the dowries: "Christ has perfect vision, fruition, and joy. Now these are the dowries." Therefore, Christ has been given these qualities as dowries.

Thomas replies that a bridegroom and a bride must, of course, be distinct people. In Christ, there is no distinction of persons between Himself and "the Son of God Who is the Bridegroom" as we see in John 3:29, where John the Baptist says of Christ, "He who has the bride is the bridegroom." Christ is not both bridegroom and bride.

As for the objections we reviewed, Thomas explains that the word "Church" has two senses. Sometimes, it describes only the body, which is united to Christ, the Head. In this sense, the Church is like a spouse, but Christ is not a member of the Church, "but is the Head from which all members receive." In the second sense, "Church" refers to the Head and the members united together, as a bridegroom to a bride. In this sense, Christ is called a member of the Church (though this expression is used imperfectly, "since a member implies a certain restriction, whereas in Christ spiritual good is not restricted but is absolutely entire … so that He is the entire good of the Church"). Yet in their union, the bride and the bridegroom become one. Therefore, while Christ can be called a member of the Church in a certain sense, He cannot be called a member of the bride, and "therefore the idea of a dowry is not becoming to Him."

As for the claim that Christ possesses the powers or gifts of the dowries, Thomas explains that this argument is faulty. It employs "a fallacy of 'accident'; for these things are not befitting to Christ if we consider them under the aspect of dowry."[94]

---

[94] That is, not all who possess similar powers possess them for the same reason. Christ has absolutely perfect vision, fruition, and

Will the angels receive a dowry?

Spiritual marriage consists of spiritual union. The spiritual union of the angels with God is not less than that between beatified men and God. Therefore, since dowries are assigned by spiritual marriage, angels should receive them too. Such is one argument from those who believe angels will receive a dowry.

Thomas replies by citing Origen's commentary on the Canticles,[95] wherein he discusses the bridegroom, the bride, the maidens, and the companions of the bridegroom. He identifies this last group with the angels. As dowries are due only to brides (the saints), it is not fitting for the companions (the angels) to receive them. Further, Christ espoused the Church through His Incarnation and Passion. We see this foreshadowed in Exodus 4:25 when Zipporah says to Moses: "Surely you are a bridegroom of blood to me!" Christ's Incarnation and Passion did not unite Him to the angels in any new way, but only to man. Therefore, the angels are not members of the Church "if we consider the Church as spouse."

Thomas explains that the angels, "without any doubt," are fit to receive any endowments that may be given to men, but not "under the aspect of a dowry," as befits a spouse. Even in spiritual marriage, a bride and bridegroom must be of the same species. This means that only man, and not the angels, is fit to be united spousally to Christ.

---

joy as God and because He is God. He does not have them in the restricted sense that glorified human beings do, and He does not have them because they have been given to Him the way they have been given to glorified human beings (as additional adornments).

[95] The Song of Solomon in the RSVCE.

Are there three dowries of the soul?

The Fathers and Doctors of the Church described three dowries of the soul in heaven: *vision*, *love*, and *fruition*.[96] Still, some think this idea unfit for several reasons. For one thing, the dowries have been said to correspond to the theological virtues of faith, hope, and charity, "whereby God Himself is the object." Now love corresponds to charity and vision to faith, but fruition also corresponds to charity, which leaves nothing to correspond to hope. Others cite a statement from Augustine that "in that beatitude God will be seen unendingly, loved without wearying, and praised untiringly." Therefore, *praise* should also be listed among the dowries.

Thomas responds that all the teachers of the Church agreed on three dowries of the soul, but differed in how they reckoned them. Some listed *vision*, *love*, and *fruition*; others, *vision*, *comprehension*, and *fruition*; still others, *vision*, *delight*, and *comprehension*. These all amount to the same things.

Next, Thomas explains that a dowry is something inherent to the soul that directs it to "the operation in which beatitude exists." Two things are required for this operation: (1) its *essence*, which is *vision*, and (2) its *perfection*, which is *delight*.[97] Further, vision is delightful in two ways: (1) on the part of the *object*, in that the thing seen is itself delightful, and (2) on the part of the *vision*, in that the act of seeing is itself delightful. We delight in seeing and knowing even evil things, not because those things themselves are delightful, but because by seeing them, we exercise our powers of vision and knowledge.

---

[96] *Visio, dilectio, et fruitio* in Latin.

[97] We might consider here that the term "Beatific Vision" itself denotes a *vision* that produces delight or happiness (*beatitude*).

Now, the Beatific Vision must be perfect, so vision must be made perfect in both ways. To be made perfect on the part of the vision, "it needs to be made connatural to the seer by means of a habit;[98] while for it to be delightful on the part of the visible object, two things are necessary": first, that the visible object be *suitable*, and second, that it be *united to the seer*.

For the vision to be delightful on its own part, we require the habit to elicit the vision, which is the *dowry* of *vision*. As for the *object*, two things are necessary: (1) it must be suitable regarding the *affections*. In this respect, "some reckon love as a dowry, others fruition (in so far as fruition regards the affective part) since what we love most we deem most suitable." (2) "Union is required on the part of the visible object," which is why some use the term "comprehension," "which is nothing else than to have God present and to hold Him within ourself." Others use the term "fruition," which does not refer to the fruition of hope, which we have while on the way to heaven, but the fruition of possession, "which is in heaven."

In this way, *the dowries do correspond to the three theological virtues*: vision corresponds to faith, comprehension (or fruition, in some sense) corresponds to hope, and fruition (or delight) corresponds to charity. "For perfect fruition such as will be had in heaven includes delight and comprehension, for which reason some take it for the one, and some for the other."

The unending *praise* of which Augustine speaks is *not a disposition* to beatitude, as are the dowries, but a *result* of beatitude. As Thomas so vividly puts it, when the soul obtains union with God, "wherein beatitude consists, it follows that the soul breaks forth into praise."

---

[98] We must be given the disposition or capacity to exercise perfect vision.

33

How Some Will Merit Another Golden Crown

Man's essential reward, which is his beatitude, consists
in the perfect union of the soul with God, inasmuch as
it enjoys God perfectly as seen and loved perfectly. Now
this reward is called a crown or aurea metaphorically.

—ST, Supplement, 96, 1

I imagine everyone reading these words has seen religious art depicting saints with golden or luminous aureoles (haloes) over their heads, but I doubt very many have come across any theological discussions of the nature of the aureoles awarded to saints in heaven. By the thirteenth century, a great deal of tradition had accrued regarding these heavenly crowns. Indeed, in his detailed treatment of the aureoles in question 96 of the Supplement, over the course of thirteen articles, Thomas cites multiple books from the Old and New Testaments, along with Church Fathers and Doctors including Ambrose, Augustine, Aymo, Bede, Bernard, Boethius, Cyprian, Dionysius, Gregory, Isidore, and Jerome. To cut through the complexity and keep our chapter to a reasonable length, we will dispense with the specific objections (fifty-nine in total) and zoom in on the gist of Thomas's answers concerning the heavenly crowns born by the saints — including our own

Angelic Doctor. Finally, to make matters simpler still, we will begin each answer with a simple yes or no, and then let Thomas flesh them out a bit.

Is an aureole the same as the essential reward, called the aurea?

No. Thomas explains that our *essential* reward in heaven is the *Beatific Vision*, which consists in the perfect union of the soul with God, who is seen and loved perfectly. This reward has been metaphorically called an *aurea* (crown) "both with reference to merit which is gained by a kind of conflict—since 'the life of man upon earth is a warfare' (Job. 7:1)[99]—and with reference to the reward whereby in a way man is made a participator of the Godhead, and consequently endowed with regal power: 'Thou has made us to our God a kingdom,' etc. (Apocalypse 5:10);[100] for a crown is the proper sign of regal power."

While all in heaven will receive their aurea, or crown, of victory, the *aureole* is an additional crown awarded only to some. It is something added to the aurea, "a kind of joy, to wit, in the works one has done, in that they have the character of a signal victory." In the book of Exodus, we read, "Thou shalt also make a little golden crown,"[101] or *coronam aureolam* (25:25). A gloss explains, "This crown denotes the new hymn which

---

[99] RSVCE: "Has not a man a hard service upon earth … ?"
[100] RSVCE: "And hast made them a kingdom and priests to our God."
[101] RSVCE: "You shall overlay it with pure gold, and make a molding of gold around it. And you shall make around it a frame a handbreadth wide, and a molding of gold around the frame" (vv. 24–25).

the virgins sing in the presence of the Lamb." "Wherefore," says Thomas, "apparently the aureole is a crown awarded, not to all, but especially to some: whereas the aurea is awarded to all the blessed."

Does the aureole differ from the fruit (Matt. 13:23)?

Yes. Thomas explains that spiritual metaphors can be used in various ways depending on the properties of the physical thing to which the spiritual life is compared. Fruits have been used in this way in several different senses. Fruits have sweetness, refresh us, and are sometimes used to describe our enjoyment of our last end with God, as we saw last chapter in our discussion of the dowry of *fruition*, because "we are said to enjoy [frui] God perfectly in heaven, and imperfectly on the way." Sometimes, fruit refers not to the last end, but to things that refresh us, such as the virtues, since "they refresh the mind with genuine sweetness," according to Ambrose. These are the fruits of the Holy Spirit, such as charity and joy, listed in Galatians 5:22. The fruits we are addressing here are fruits in yet another spiritual sense.

We read in Matthew 13:23 that Christ divided the fruits of seeds into thirtyfold, sixtyfold, and hundredfold yields. Christ refers to the spiritual seed (the Word of God) sown within us, which gives us a particular spirituality as we withdraw from carnal, worldly things. The greater the withdrawal, "the greater is the fruit of the Word" in us. So "the 'aurea' consists in the joy one has in God, and the 'aureole' in the joy one has in the perfection of one's works, whereas the 'fruit' consists in the joy that the worker has in his own disposition as to his degree of spirituality to which he has attained through the seed of God's Word."

Further, various awards may correspond to the same merit for various reasons. For example, virginity corresponds to the *aurea* in that it is kept for God's sake at the command of charity; to the *aureole* in that it is a work of perfection representing a signal victory over the flesh; and to the *fruit* because the virgin "acquires a certain spirituality by withdrawing from carnal things."

Is a fruit due to the virtue of continence alone?

Yes. Thomas cites a gloss on Matthew 13:23 that indicates the "hundredfold" fruit is awarded to virginity, the "sixtyfold" to widowhood, and the "thirtyfold" to conjugal (marital) continence. Fruits are rewards for passing from the carnal life to the spiritual life, so a fruit corresponds especially to the virtue that frees us from subjection to the flesh. This is seen foremostly in the virtue of continence, since the lures of sexual pleasures are the most powerful.

Do the fruits correspond to the three parts of continence: virginity, widowhood, and marital chastity?

Yes. Thomas notes that a certain spirituality is necessary, and another is "superabundant." It is necessary to possess a spirituality that is not disturbed by pleasures of the flesh, but partakes in carnal pleasure only "according to the order of right reason. This is the spirituality of married persons." Superabundant spirituality is seen when a person withdraws entirely from carnal pleasures "which stifle the spirit." If this is done in respect to all times, past, present, and future, this is the spirituality of virgins, and if this is done at a particular time, this is the spirituality of widows.

Is an aureole awarded to holy virgins?

Yes. God says, "To the eunuchs who keep my sabbaths ... I will give in my house and within my walls a monument and a name better than sons and daughters" (Isa. 56:4, 5). A gloss explains, "This refers to their peculiar and transcendent glory." Virgins are the "eunuchs who have made themselves eunuchs for the sake of the kingdom of heaven" described in Matthew 19:12. "Therefore it would seem," says Thomas, "that some special reward is due to virginity, and this called the aureole." Aureoles are given for special, signal victories. We know that "the desires of the flesh are against the Spirit" (Gal. 5:17), so a special crown is due for the spiritual victory of virginity.

Do martyrs receive an aureole?

Yes. Thomas declares that just as the special crown we call the aureole is duly rewarded to virgins for their most perfect victory over concupiscence (tendency to sin) of the flesh, so too such an aureole is due for the martyrs' most perfect victory over external assaults, whereby the irascible passions (which goad us to fight back or flee from bodily attacks) are conquered.

Are doctors (holy teachers) awarded an aureole?

Yes. Just as virgins and martyrs obtain most perfect victories over the flesh and the world, so too do holy preachers and teachers win a most perfect victory over the devil. Indeed, not only do they refuse to yield to the devil's assault, but they drive him out of others by teaching the things of salvation. Indeed, this is a signal victory in spiritual warfare. As we read in 2 Corinthians 10:4, "The weapons of our warfare are not worldly but have divine power." Thomas notes, too, that this aureole is not only for prelates or people of high ecclesiastical authority, but for anyone who lawfully teaches and preaches the gospel. Further, simply being a prelate with the capacity and office to preach does not merit an aureole, unless one actually preaches, "since a crown is not due to the habit, but to the actual strife." As we read in 2 Timothy 2:5, "An athlete is not crowned unless he competes according to the rules."

Is an aureole due to Christ?

No. The aureoles reward our *conformity* to Christ through virginity, martyrdom, or teaching. An *aureole,* by its very name as a diminutive of "aurea," "denotes something possessed by participation and not in its fullness." In Christ, "the notion of victory is found chiefly and fully, for by His victory others are made victors," as we read in John 16:33: "Be of good cheer, I have overcome the world." Further, we read in Revelation 5:5 that "the Lion of the tribe of Judah, the Root of David, has conquered." Christ does not receive an aureole, but is the source from which they flow.

Do angels receive an aureole?

Again, no. As we saw in the last section, "an athlete is not crowned unless he competes according to the rules" (2 Tim. 2:5). Angels do not compete or suffer conflict as we do. Further, aureoles reward acts performed in the body, and angels are bodiless, spiritual beings. The things that produce perfect merit in man are natural to the angels, so they will not have aureoles in the same sense that humans will.

Is an aureole also due to the body?

No, but ... Since the separated souls now in heaven already have aureoles, the proper subject of an aureole is the soul, not the body. Further, all merit arises from the soul, so the whole reward should exist in the soul. Strictly speaking, "the aureole is in the mind: since it is joy in the works to which an aureole is due." Still, even as the joy of the aurea, the essential reward, produces a certain comeliness in the body, the aureole results in bodily comeliness "so that the aureole is chiefly in the mind, but by a kind of overflow it shines forth in the body."

Are three aureoles fittingly assigned to
virgins, martyrs, and doctors?

Yes. We have seen that virginity signifies a victory over the *flesh*, martyrdom conquers persecution coming from the *world*, and teaching and preaching achieve victory over the *devil* regarding not only one's own soul, but also the souls of others. Further, teachers and preachers are conformed to Christ in that He, as a teacher, was the mediator between man and the Father and proclaimed the truth to the world. Christ was a martyr in suffering the persecution of the world, and in His personal purity, He was a virgin. For the special ways that virgins, martyrs, and doctors conform to Christ, they receive fitting aureoles.

Is the virgin's aureole the greatest of all?

No, not necessarily. We do read in the book of Revelation that virgins "follow the Lamb wherever he goes," and that "no one could learn" the song before God's throne except them (14:4, 3). Further, St. Cyprian (ca. A.D. 200–258) called virgins "the more illustrious portion of Christ's flock." Still, we can consider one aureole's excellence over that of others from two different standpoints. If we look at aureoles in terms of "the things about which the battle is fought," the doctor's aureole would take precedence, because the conflict regards intelligible, spiritual goods, while the conflicts faced by the virgins and martyrs concern sensible, bodily passions.

The more important standpoint, however, considers the strenuousness and dangers of the conflicts themselves, since it is more difficult to achieve victory over greater hardships. In this regard, the martyr's aureole is simply the greatest of all. Matthew 5:10 gives us the eighth beatitude: "Blessed are those who are persecuted for righteousness' sake, for theirs is the kingdom of heaven." A gloss says that "all the other beatitudes are perfected in the eighth, which refers to the martyrs." This is also why the Church, when classing saints as martyrs, virgins, and doctors, places the martyrs first. Still, "nothing hinders the other aureoles from being more excellent in some particular way."

Can one person's aureole be more excellent than another's?

Yes. The aureoles are given in addition to the aurea. Some people have a more intense aurea (beatitude) than others, and the same holds for the aureoles. Since merit is involved in the cause of reward, different degrees of merit warrant different levels of reward. Further, "the merit of an aureole may be intensified in two ways: first, on the part of its cause, secondly on the part of the work." Thomas asks us to consider two men who are martyred. The first man possesses less charity than the second, but he suffers more during his martyrdom. The second man will have a greater aurea for his greater degree of charity, while the first man, who merits less in his essential reward (aurea), may receive a greater aureole for his martyrdom. Similarly, one virgin may have withdrawn from carnal temptation to a greater extent than another, and will therefore be awarded a greater aureole. "Nothing hinders one aureole being more excellent than another."

34

Last Thoughts on the Last Things: Heaven

*Heaven is the ultimate end and fulfillment
of the deepest human longings, the state
of supreme, definitive happiness.*

—CCC 1024

Paragraphs 1023–1029 of the *Catechism* briefly describe various aspects of heaven: how we will see God face-to-face and live a perfect life of love with the Trinity, the Blessed Mother, the angels, and all the blessed; how Christ opened heaven's gates for us; and how those of us in heaven will revel forever in the glorious, joyful contemplation of God known as the Beatific Vision. Thomas, as we have seen, has given us much more to contemplate about the various mysteries, joys, and rewards of heaven that should inspire us to experience them firsthand when we look upon the face of God.

As the first of my last thoughts, I would like to note the absurdity of the idea that heaven is a boring place. More than one modern lyricist has written about the foreboding tediousness of strumming harps forever in heaven, and many satirists have expressed their preference for laughing with the sinners in hell rather than crying with the saints in heaven. Hopefully, you have seen that these writers should peruse the lines of St. Thomas on the supreme joys of heaven!

Augustine famously wrote of God that "our heart is restless until it rests in you." While all the diverse things and pleasures of the earth are good because they exist and come from God, they can never satisfy us fully or for very long. Early in his great *Summa*, Thomas eloquently makes clear that the goodness of every created thing—from the simple beauty of a flower or a newborn babe, to the glorious majesty of the sun, to the unfathomable vastness of a universe with countless galaxies visible at night—participates in the ultimate, total goodness of God:

> He produced many and diverse creatures, that what was wanting to one in the representation of the divine goodness might be supplied by another. For goodness, which in God is simple and uniform, in creatures is manifold and divided and hence the whole universe together participates in the divine goodness more perfectly, and represents it better than any single creature.[102]

We see this expressed in Scripture as well: "From the greatness and beauty of created things comes a corresponding perception of their Creator" (Wisd. 13:5). This is why Thomas's own great teacher, St. Albert the Great (ca. 1200–1280) proclaimed, "The whole world is theology for us because the heavens proclaim the glory of God."[103] So the goodness of seeing God face-to-face in His essence in heaven will so far exceed the combined total of

---

[102] *ST*, I, 47, 1.

[103] From St. Albert's commentary on the Gospel of Matthew, cited in Paul Murray, *The New Wine of Dominican Spirituality: A Drink Called Happiness* (New York: Burns and Oates, 2006), 93.

every limited good thing we have ever experienced that we can hardly imagine it.

Moreover, as Thomas has made clear, God has additional, even more wondrous gifts in store for us. Those of us who marvel at the beauty of the galaxies will view them with glorified eyes that see farther and more clearly than ever before, and, through the powers of subtlety and agility, will be able to travel to them in an instant. Moreover, after the celestial bodies have been renewed, all their wonders will shine as never before.[104]

We should also consider Thomas's insights on how both body and soul are rewarded in heaven. He says the superabundance of our spiritual joy will overflow into the body. As for the potential boredom of "strumming harps" forever, think of a time when you were so relieved of a great burden, or received such joyous news, that you could not help but cry out "Hallelujah!" or "Thank you, God!" As Augustine and Thomas have explained, our heavenly joy will be so great that we will spontaneously burst out with joyful praise, joining the choirs of angels in heaven as they sing, "Holy, holy, holy, is the Lord God Almighty" (Rev. 4:8).

Note, too, that Thomas describes degrees of happiness and differing heavenly "mansions," "aureoles," and "fruits" that we will receive in different measure. We will attain additional "small crowns" (aureoles) and "fruits" as gifts from God according to our state in life, whether we were faithful married persons, celibate widows, virgins, martyrs, or teachers. All in heaven will receive that great crown, the aurea of the Beatific Vision of God. Even

---

[104] Particularly attentive readers may recall Thomas's explanation that the delight we take in vision comes from both the exercise of the power of vision itself and the beauty of the objects we see. In heaven, we will see, with greater clarity than ever before, objects more beautiful than we can now imagine!

in that regard, although every person's aurea will be the greatest boon he could possibly receive, it will vary in its degree or intensity of joy and fulfillment. This variance will correspond to the degree that each of us, while alive, chose to accept God's loving charity; to forbear the lures of the flesh, the world, and the devil; and to grow in union with God. The more we bear Christ's yoke of love on earth, the lighter will be our burden and the higher we will rise in heaven.

Part 4

To Hell for Those Who Choose It

In due sequence we must consider those things that concern
the damned after the judgment: (1) The punishment of
the damned, and the fire by which their bodies will be
tormented; (2) matters relating to their will and intellect;
(3) God's justice and mercy in regard to the damned.

—*ST*, Supplement, 97, Prologue

35

On the Punishment of the Damned

This is also becoming to Divine justice, that whereas they departed from one by sin, and placed their end in material things which are many and various, so should they be tormented in many ways and from many sources.

—*ST*, Supplement, 97, 1

Is fire the only punishment in hell?

According to Matthew 25:41, at the Last Judgment, Christ will say to those who died in mortal sin: "Depart from me, you cursed, into the eternal fire." Further, fire is the punishment for venial sins in purgatory: "The fire will test what sort of work each one has done" (1 Cor. 3:13). Hence, some believe fire will be the sole punishment for sins in hell.

Thomas replies, to the contrary, "On the wicked he will rain coals of fire and brimstone; a scorching wind shall be the portion of their cup" (Ps. 11 [10]:6). Further, "drought and heat snatch away the snow waters; so does Sheol those who have sinned" (Job 24:19). Thomas continues with insights from St. Basil of Caesarea, who wrote that at the final cleansing of the world, the elements will be separated. All that is pure and noble will remain above "for the glory of the blessed," while all that is ignoble and sordid will be cast down to punish and torment the damned. Indeed, we read in Wisdom 5:21–23 that lightning, hailstones, seas, rivers, and mighty winds will rage against evildoers.

As we saw in our opening quotation, it is becoming to divine justice for sinners, who chose to depart from the one God and place their ends in diverse material things, to be tormented by a variety of material things. Because fire produces the most pain, it is used to denote any intense torment.

As for the objections, Thomas notes that the fire of purgatory is not intended primarily to torment, but to cleanse, so it cannot be directly compared to the punishing fire of hell.

Is the "worm of the damned" corporeal?

Scripture tells us that the damned will be punished with fire and worms (Jth. 16:17;[105] Sir. 7:17[106]). Also, Augustine wrote that the fire and worms will punish the body. For these reasons, some think that in hell, the damned will be tortured by actual, physical worms.

Thomas begins by noting that Augustine acknowledged differing opinions on the issue, but considered it most likely that fire would afflict the *body literally*, and the worm would affect the *soul metaphorically*. Thomas notes that after the judgment, the only mixed bodies (composites of body and soul) that will remain are human beings, since only humans have immaterial and immortal souls. No animals, including worms, will exist. The

---

[105] Verse 21 in the Latin version Thomas used and in the Douay-Rheims translation.

[106] Verse 19 in Thomas's Latin Bible and in the Douay-Rheims translation. In both, the book of Sirach is called "Ecclesiasticus."

worm referred to in Scripture is not corporeal, but spiritual. "This is the remorse of conscience, which is called a worm because it originates from the corruption of sin, and torments the soul, as a corporeal worm born of corruption torments by gnawing."

Will the damned weep real tears?

We read in Luke 13:28, "There you will weep and gnash your teeth."[107] A gloss indicates that this text proves the resurrection of the body, which would not be the case if the weeping were merely spiritual and not physical.

Thomas replies that corporeal, bodily weeping "results from dissolving into tears." This is not possible in the damned, because they do not eat or drink, their bodies, being of finite quantity, cannot continually restore what is lost in tears. Besides, bodies will not generate or be corrupted after Judgment Day. Still, bodily weeping also denotes "a certain commotion and disturbance of the head and eyes, and in this respect weeping will be possible in the damned after the resurrection." Though they will not shed physical tears, the bodies of the damned will be tormented both from without and from within, since the body will be affected by "the soul's passion towards good or evil. In this sense, weeping is a proof of the body's resurrection, and it corresponds to the pleasure of sin, experienced by both soul and body."

Are the damned in material darkness?

Some think the damned will not live in darkness because they would not be able to see their own punishment. Further, when

---

[107] See also Matthew 13:42.

reunited with their bodies, the damned will have the power of vision, which would be useless without the light necessary for sight.

Thomas responds that it is "in the outer darkness" that the damned will be cast to weep and gnash their teeth (Matt. 22:13). He cites Gregory's argument that the fire of hell will not give light; otherwise, the damned "would by no means be described as cast into exterior darkness." Thomas also cites St. Basil of Caesarea's argument that "by God's might the brightness of the fire will be separated from its power of burning, so that its brightness will conduce to the joy of the blessed, and the heat of the flame to the torment of the damned."

Thomas elaborates that the conditions in hell provide the utmost torment to the damned, so that there will be both light and darkness insofar as they contribute to punishment. While, as Aristotle notes, sight usually provides us pleasure, it brings us pain when what we see is painful to us and displeasing to our will. So in hell, there will be only dim light, so that "nothing be seen clearly, and that only such things be dimly seen as are able to bring anguish to the heart. Wherefore, simply speaking, the place is dark."

Will there be physical fire in hell?

Some cite St. John Damascene, Augustine, or Gregory to argue that there will not be physical fire in hell. St. John Damascene wrote that the everlasting fire will be "not material fire, such as that which we have, but such as God knoweth." Augustine wrote that in his opinion, "the place to which the soul is committed after death is spiritual and not corporeal." Gregory wrote that there is "but one hell fire, but it does not torture all sinners equally," and "each one will suffer as much pain according as his guilt deserves." Therefore, some reason, the fire will not be corporeal (physical).

Thomas begins his response with further clarification from Gregory himself, who wrote, "I doubt not that the fire of hell is corporeal, since it is certain that bodies are tortured there." Thomas then moves into a philosophical and theological discussion of the nature of hell, describing primarily the theories of Avicenna, who thought only souls would be punished after death, and explaining that the shortcomings of that view. Thomas says both soul and body are punished, and he notes that Augustine also wrote that "the fire by which the bodies are tormented is corporeal."

As for the objections, St. John Damascene did not deny that the fire was material, only that it differs from ours in some of its properties. Augustine's comment can be taken to mean that after death, souls are taken to a place that can be described as incorporeal, because the soul is not there corporeally, but spiritually, as are the angels. Most interestingly, Thomas notes as well that "we may reply that Augustine is expressing an opinion without deciding the point, as he often does in those books."[108] As for Gregory's comment, while fire by itself will not be able to generate pain commensurate with a person's sin, it can do so as "regulated by the ordering of Divine justice: even so the fire of the furnace is regulated by the forethought of the smith, according as the effect of his art requires."

---

[108] "Those books" being Augustine's commentary on Genesis, *De Genesi ad Litteram.*

Is the fire of hell just like ours?

Those who argue that the fire of hell cannot possibly be like the fire we know cite the following sources (in the order of the four objections):

1. Augustine wrote that in his opinion, "no man knows of what kind is the everlasting fire, unless the Spirit of God has revealed it to anyone." But we all know the nature of earthly fire.
2. Gregory wrote that earthly fire requires fuel, but the fires of hell burn eternally with no kind of kindling.
3. Aristotle wrote that the everlasting and the corruptible differ essentially. We know that our fire is corruptible, and Christ proclaimed that the fire of hell is everlasting (Matt. 25:41).
4. Our fire gives light, yet we read in Job 18:5 that "the flame of [the wicked's] fire does not shine."

Thomas begins his response with another passage from Aristotle: "Every water is of the same species as every other water." This would also hold for the element of fire, so that "every fire is of the same species as every other fire." Further, we read in Wisdom 11:16 that "one is punished by the very things by which he sins." Since people sin through the sensible things of the world, it is just that they should be punished by the same things.

Thomas notes that fire itself is always of essentially the same kind of species, but the kind of matter that feeds it can differ in species: "Wherefore flame and burning coal differ specifically, and likewise burning wood and red-hot iron." The fire of hell is of the same species or nature as our fire: "But whether that fire subsists in its proper matter, or if it subsists in a strange matter, what that matter may be, we know not."

As for Thomas's replies to the objections:

1. Augustine is referring to fire's matter and not its nature.

2. Our fire, as Gregory notes, does require fuel and is kindled by man, but the fire of hell needs neither fuel nor foreign matter to keep it alive, because "it is kindled not by man but by God, Who fashioned its nature." We know this from Isaiah 30:33: "The breath of the LORD, like a stream of brimstone, kindles it."

3. Just as the bodies of the damned, once corruptible, will be made everlasting by God's power in accord with divine justice, so too will the fire of hell be made incorruptible.

4. As flames on earth do not shine brightly when obscured by thick smoke or opaque substances, such as sulfur, so too the fires of hell will not burn brightly.

Is the fire of hell beneath the earth?

Job 18:18 says, "He is thrust from light into darkness, and driven out of the world." Some take this to mean that the fire in which the damned will be punished is not beneath the earth, but outside of it. Further, we read in Ecclesiastes 1:15 that "what is lacking cannot be numbered." Since the damned will be vast in number, the space that holds their bodies must exceed the capacity of the hollow within the earth. Finally, since, as we saw in our last section, "one is punished by the very things by which he sins" (Wisd. 11:16), the wicked who sinned *on* earth will not be punished by fire *beneath* it.

Thomas responds that there are many reasons to conclude that the fire of hell is actually beneath us. In Isaiah 14:9, we read, "Sheol beneath is stirred up to meet you when you come." Gregory wrote, "I see not what hinders us from believing that hell is beneath the earth." Moreover, a gloss on Jonah 2:3[109] notes that the "heart of the seas" into which he was cast represents hell. The phrase "the heart of the earth" (Matt. 12:40) has "the same sense, for as the heart is in the middle of an animal, so is hell supposed to be in the middle of the earth."

While Augustine and Gregory did not claim to know for sure the location of hell, and some believed it could be on the earth's surface, Gregory believed it was most likely located beneath the earth. We call hell "the nether regions" (*infernus*[110]) because it is beneath us (*inferius*). Moreover, we read in Revelation 5:3 that "no one in heaven or on earth or under the earth was able to open the scroll or to look into it." Heaven refers to the angels; earth, to man; and under the earth, to the souls in hell.

As an interesting aside, Thomas notes that according to Aristotle, the philosopher Pythagoras "held the place of punishment to be in a fiery sphere … in the middle of the whole world: and he called it the prison house of Jupiter…. It is, however, more in keeping with Scripture to say that it is beneath the earth." [111]

---

[109] Jonas 2:4 in the *ST* and Douay-Rheims.

[110] The Latin word for hell.

[111] Quite interestingly, too, modern scientists describe Earth's core as extremely hot, nearly as hot as the sun, and of incredible density. Speaking of almost unthinkable density, Thomas notes, without offering his own judgment, that "some hold that this darkness is caused by the massing together of the bodies of the damned, which will so fill the place of hell with their numbers, that no air will remain, so that there will be no translucid body that can be the subject of light and darkness, except for the eyes of the damned, which will be darkened utterly" (*ST*, Supplement, 97, 4).

As for the objections, Job 18:18 means that God removes the wicked from the earth's *surface*. Thomas notes that "hell is accounted one of the three things that 'never are satisfied'" (Prov. 30:15–16), so it will not run out of space. By God's power, hell can hold all the bodies of the damned "within the bowels of the earth." Finally, man is punished by the very things by which he sinned, not in the sense that he is punished in "the very place where he sinned," but "for as much as man having sinned in soul and body will be punished in both."

36

Of the Will and Intellect of the Damned

Envy reigns supreme in the damned.

—ST, Supplement, 98, 4

Do the damned will only evil?

Dionysius argued that "evil is altogether involuntary," and "the demons desire the good and the best, namely, to be, to live, to understand." Further, some of the damned, such as certain heathens, will have acquired natural, civic virtues while on earth, and through virtuous habits, the will "elicits praiseworthy acts." Therefore, it seems to some that the damned can still will what is good.

Thomas responds that the kind of obstinate will that rejects God "can never be inclined except to evil." Indeed, the will of the damned relates to evil just as the will of the blessed relates to good. The blessed can never will evil, and the damned can never will good.

Thomas clarifies that the damned have "a twofold will." Through the Author of nature, they possess a *natural* will, which inclines them to some sort of good, and will remain in them. It is through the *deliberate* will, however, that we can choose the things to which our affections incline us. The deliberate will of the damned is always evil, because they have turned away from God, "the last end of a right will," and they never will true good.

Evil as evil does not draw the will; only the perceived good can. In their wickedness, the damned value what is evil as though it were good. In speaking of the demons, Dionysius refers to the natural, not the deliberate will. The demons desire good by their natural will, but their deliberate will is corrupted by their wickedness. The civic life does not continue after this life, and natural, civic virtues do not remain in separated souls after death. Even if they were to remain, the damned would never actually exercise them, "being enchained, as it were, by the obstinacy of the mind."

Do the damned repent of the evil they have done?

Some think the damned will never repent for the evil they have done, since, as we read in Proverbs 2:14, they "rejoice in doing evil and delight in the perverseness of evil." Further, repentance would require a good will, and we just saw that the damned will only evil.

Thomas first responds with the words of Wisdom 5:3 regarding the wicked: "They will speak to one another in repentance." Further, Aristotle notes that from a natural perspective, "the wicked are full of repentance" in the sense that they later feel sorrow for the evil pleasures they enjoyed.

Thomas explains that a person may repent of sin in two ways, either directly or indirectly. One who repents directly hates the sin itself, and one who repents indirectly hates the sin because of something else, namely, the punishment it has brought. The damned will indeed hate their punishment, and so they will repent, but only indirectly. They will not repent for the shamefulness of vice itself, which is an act of good will.

Will the damned, with right reason, prefer not to exist?

Building upon some statements from Augustine, some argue that the damned could never reasonably wish not to exist rather than to endure their punishment. The greater an evil, the more it is to be avoided. Not to be is the greatest of all evils, since it contains no good whatsoever, not even the goodness of existence.

To the contrary, Thomas responds with the words of Revelation 9:6: "In those days men will seek death and will not find it; they will long to die, and death will fly from them." Since the unhappiness of the damned exceeds all earthly unhappiness, it would indeed be reasonable for them to desire not to exist. Sirach 41:2 says, "O death, how welcome is your sentence to one who is in need and is failing in strength, very old and distracted over everything; to one who is contrary, and has lost his patience!" All the more so will *not to be* seem preferable to the damned.

Thomas clarifies that not to be can be understood in two ways: *in itself* or *as a relief* from ongoing pain and unhappiness. The first can never be reasonably desired, because it contains no good, but is in fact the complete lack or privation of good. In the second sense, not to be "takes on the aspect of good," since per Aristotle, "to lack an evil is a kind of good." In this sense, it would be preferable for the damned not to be rather than to be perpetually unhappy. Thus we read of Judas in Matthew 26:24: "Woe to that man by whom the Son of man is betrayed! It would have been better for that man if he had not been born."

Will the damned desire the damnation of others?

It may seem that the damned do *not* necessarily wish others to be damned. We read, for example, that the rich man in the Gospel prayed that his brothers would not join him in Hades (Luke 16:27–28). Further, the damned still retain their improper, inordinate affections, and they would not wish for the damnation of those they loved inordinately. Lastly, the damned would not wish to increase their own suffering, which is the case when others are damned, just as the joy of the blessed is increased when others join their number.

To the contrary, Thomas references Isaiah 14:9, which says the shades in Sheol, even kings, rise and greet those who have joined them. A gloss on that verse says: "The wicked are comforted by having many companions in their punishment."[112] Further, in a most memorable statement of his own, Thomas declares that "envy reigns supreme in the damned."

Thomas elaborates that as the blessed in heaven possess the most perfect charity, the damned in hell possess the most perfect hate. Hate is embodied in envy. As love rejoices in the good of others, so envy causes suffering at the sight of another's joy. The sight of the happiness of the saints will cause great pain to the damned, as we read in Isaiah 26:11: "Let the envious people see and be confounded, and let fire devour Thy enemies."[113]

As for the objections, the envy of the wicked is so great and their unhappiness so severe that they will envy even the glory of their kinfolk. Still, they will envy their kin less than others, since

---

[112] This may call to mind the well-known aphorism "Misery loves company."

[113] RSVCE: "Let them see thy zeal for thy people, and be ashamed. Let the fire for thy adversaries consume them."

their unhappiness would increase if their own family were damned along with them, while others of no relation to them are saved. In this sense, a damned person might pray that his brothers are saved, while "he would rather that his brethren were damned as well as all the rest." As for the inordinate love of worldly things, Aristotle notes that such love is easily blotted out. The damned will preserve no friendships. Finally, even though as more people are damned, the punishment of each damned person increases, the hatred and envy of the damned be so great that they will indeed prefer to be tormented with as many others as possible, rather than to bear their torment alone.

Do the damned hate God?

It may seem that the damned do not, and indeed cannot, hate God, since Dionysius has made clear that "the beautiful and good that is the cause of all goodness and beauty is beloved of all," and this cause is God. Further, one can neither hate goodness of itself nor will evil in itself, as we saw before that "evil is altogether involuntary."

Thomas shows, however, that the damned will indeed hate God. As Psalm 74 [73]:23 says, "The impious scoff at thee all the day!" Our desires are moved by good or evil as we apprehend them, and we apprehend God in two ways: first, *in Himself*, as the blessed see Him in His essence, and second, *in His effects*, as we and the damned see Him. Now, since His essence is goodness itself, no one who sees His essence can hate Him. On the other hand, those who experience displeasure because of His effects can therefore hate Him. In other words, the damned see God in His punishment, which is the effect of divine justice, and "hate Him, even as they hate the punishment inflicted on them."

Dionysius's first statement refers to the natural appetite, which has become distorted and perverse in the damned through the choices of their deliberate will. His second statement would be true only if the damned saw God in His essence, which they do not.

Do the damned demerit and earn more punishment?

Some think they do. The damned are on equal footing with the demons, and the serpent who tempted man to sin received further punishment from God (Gen. 3:14–15). Further, an evil act that proceeds from another deliberate act of the will is not excused. Aristotle notes that a man who commits a crime while drunk is not excused from his crime, but actually deserves a *double punishment,* for drinking to the point of drunkenness and for the crime that followed. Since the damned are in hell because of their obstinacy, further sins proceed from their free will, and they are not excused from demerit.

Thomas's replies to the contrary include the argument that "after reaching the last term" (that is, after Judgment Day), "there is no further movement, or advancement in good or evil. Now the damned ... will have reached the last term of their damnation" and "will not demerit by their perverse will, for if they did their damnation would be augmented." He notes that we must distinguish between the times before and after the Day of Judgment, because merit (or demerit) is directed to the attainment of further good (or evil), and after Judgment Day, "good and evil will have reached their ultimate consummation, so that there will be no further addition to good or evil."

As for the objections, the state of the damned does differ from that of the demons, since damned humans do not work to draw others to damnation as the demons do before the Last Judgment. Thus, demons (but not men) earn demerit in terms of secondary punishment beyond their damnation. Unlike drunken criminals, the damned do not earn a double punishment, because they have already "reached the highest of evils."

Can the damned use knowledge they had while on earth?

Reasons to think the damned will *not* be able to retain and use the knowledge they acquired on earth include the following: knowledge can provide pleasure, which the damned are incapable of experiencing; pain disturbs one's ability to think, and the damned are always distracted by pain; and as Aristotle points out, "length of time is the cause of forgetfulness," so those who are damned eternally will eventually forget everything they once knew.

Still, Thomas notes that Abraham said to the rich man in Luke 16:25, "Remember that you in your lifetime received your good things," and so forth. This means the damned will be able to think about things they knew on earth. Thomas fleshes this out with an insight from his philosophical psychology (presented in *ST*, I, 89, and briefly in chapter 2 of this book). Namely, "intelligible species," that is, knowledge stored in the intellectual soul, will remain after death, and this knowledge would be of no purpose if it could not be used.

Just as all knowledge serves to increase the joys of the saints, so too all knowledge serves to increase the sorrows of the damned. Knowledge of joyful things provides pleasure, while knowledge of grievous things increases unhappiness. The damned will consider both the evil they did that led to their damnation and the delightful goods that they have lost. Both will increase their torment.

These considerations answer the first objection. As for the second, bodily pain does distract us and hinder our ability to concentrate while here on earth, but in the future life, the soul will not be affected by the body in the same way, so that "however much the body may suffer, the soul will have a most clear view of those things that can be a cause of anguish to it." As for the forgetfulness that grows with time, in the future life, the heavens will cease to move and there will be no time as we know it. Nothing will be forgotten in eternity.

Will the damned ever think about God?

It may seem the damned think about God. As we have seen, they hate Him, and one cannot hate what one does not think about. Further, the damned will feel the remorse of the worm of conscience. Since conscience suffers for acts committed against God, the damned must think about God.

Thomas begins by noting that the most perfect thoughts concern God, and since the damned will be in a state of "greatest imperfection," they will not think about God. He elaborates that one may think about God in two ways. First, one may think of God in Himself according to what is proper to Him as the font of all goodness. One cannot think of God in this way without delight, so the damned cannot think of God in Himself. Second, one may think of God according to things accidental to Him—that is, His effects, such as His punishments. This form of thinking about God can bring sorrow, and the damned will think about Him in this way only.

As for the objections, the damned will experience hatred for God or remorse for sin because they think of Him only in terms of how He punishes them and forbids them from doing what their evil wills desire. They will not hate God in Himself or suffer remorse for their sins because they have offended Him.

Will the damned see the glory of the blessed?

Some think the damned will *not* see the glory of the blessed. The damned are more distant from the blessed than from us on earth, and the damned cannot see what happens here. As evidence, Gregory cites Job 14:21: "His sons came to honor, and he does not know; they are brought low, and he perceives it not." Further, St. Paul was granted the great favor of being "caught up into Paradise" (2 Cor. 12:3) to behold the life of the saints in heaven with God. Something granted as a great favor to the saints in this life would not be granted to the damned.

Thomas responds, however, that the rich man in hell "saw Abraham far off and Lazarus in his bosom" (Luke 16:23). He clarifies that before Judgment Day, the damned see the blessed in glory insofar as they know the blessed "are in a state of glory that surpasses all thought," although the damned do not see what that glory is like. The envy of the damned will gnaw at them as they grieve for their own unhappiness, having forfeited such glory. Wisdom 5:2 says of those who will see the righteous, "When they see him, they will be shaken with dreadful fear, and they will be amazed at his unexpected salvation." After the judgment, the damned will no longer see the blessed, though they will be forever haunted by their memory of those in the state of blessed glory. "Finding themselves deemed unworthy even to see the glory which the saints merit to have," they will suffer all the more.

As for the objections, what happens on earth during this life would not serve to torment the damned in hell as would "the sight of the glory of the saints." Hence, the things of this world are not shown to the damned, except for things that happen here that "are capable of causing them sorrow." As for St. Paul, he was granted in this life an actual experience of the life that the saints share with God, inspiring hope "to have it more perfectly in the life to come." This is nothing like the vision of the blessed given to the damned.

37

On God's Mercy and Justice
toward the Damned

*We find also other reasons given by the saints why
some are justly condemned to everlasting punishment
for a temporal sin. One is because they sinned against
an eternal good by despising eternal life.*

—ST, Supplement, 99, 1

*Is it fitting for divine justice to impose
eternal punishment on sinners?*

Some in Thomas's day, as in our own, questioned how it could
be just to punish people eternally for sins they committed during their brief time on earth. Indeed, to some, this punishment
appeared contrary not only to reason, but also to Scripture. We
read in Deuteronomy 25:2 that a man is to be punished "with a
number of stripes in proportion to his offense." This is but one
of six objections that Thomas presents.

Thomas begins his response with the clear and relevant words
of Matthew 25:46 regarding the unrighteous: "They will go away
into eternal punishment." Thomas continues with the logical
argument that "as reward is to merit, so is punishment to guilt."

Further, we know from Scripture that an eternal reward is given for the temporal merit we accrue during our earthly lives: "Every one who sees the Son and believes in him should have eternal life" (John 6:40). Aristotle also noted that "punishment is meted according to the dignity of the person sinned against," and Thomas adds that whoever sins mortally has sinned against God, whose dignity and majesty are infinite. Therefore, mortal sins deserve infinite, unending punishment.

Thomas elaborates that punishment is measured according to its *severity* and its *duration*. Now, the severity of a punishment corresponds to the severity of the fault, so that those who sin more seriously receive more grievous punishments: "As she glorified herself and played the wanton, so give her a like measure of torment and mourning" (Rev. 18:7). Still, the duration of the punishment does not correspond with the duration of the fault. Augustine noted that sins that occur in a short space of time, such as adultery, are not punished with penalties of brief duration. Even our human laws allow some heinous crimes that take little time to commit to be punished with permanent banishment or even death, thereby perpetually cutting the perpetrator off entirely from "the fellowship of the citizens."

In the same manner, Thomas says, according to divine justice, mortal sin "renders a person worthy to be altogether cut off from the fellowship of God's city, and this is the effect of every sin committed against charity, which is the bond uniting this same city together." Earthly punishments are not eternal, because the earthly state itself is not permanent; but if a person were to live forever, some human punishments would indeed last forever. Still, regarding duration of punishment, those with lesser, venial sins "as not to deserve to be entirely cut off from the fellowship of the saints" will be punished (in purgatory) for however long it takes for their sins to be cleansed.

Thomas gives other reasons, including the one given in our opening quotation, to explain the justice of eternal punishment. Augustine was among the saints who argued that an everlasting punishment is fitting for temporal sin when that sin is committed against an eternal good out of disdain for eternal life: "He is become worthy of eternal evil, who destroyed in himself a good which could be eternal." Gregory chimed in that "it belongs to the great justice of the judge that those should never cease to be punished, who in this life never ceased to desire sin." Thomas himself adds that the guilt of those who die in mortal sin will last forever, since it cannot be remitted without grace, people cannot obtain grace after death, and punishment should not end as long as guilt remains.

As for the objection based on Deuteronomy 25:2, we have seen that punishment need not match a sin in terms of its duration. Further, building upon insights from Gregory, Thomas notes that "although sin is temporal in act, it is eternal in will."

Will God's mercy one day end the punishment of demons and the damned?

We have considered God's justice, and now we will look at His mercy. Some offer scriptural and logical arguments that God's mercy will one day bring to an end the punishment of the damned and the demons. Wisdom 11:24 says, "For thou lovest all things that exist, and hast loathing for none of the things thou hast made." According to Romans 11:32, "God has consigned all men to disobedience, that he may have mercy upon all." Further, Anselm argued that "it is not just that God should permit the utter loss of a creature which He made for happiness." Therefore, in keeping with justice and mercy, the punishment of men and angels will not last forever.

Thomas begins his response once again with Christ's words regarding the unrighteous: "They will go away into eternal punishment" (Matt. 25:46). Thomas adds, most straightforwardly, "Therefore they will be punished eternally." As for the demons, just as the good angels received permanent happiness by freely turning to God, so too will the bad angels suffer eternal unhappiness as the consequence of their choice.

Thomas elaborates with words from Augustine condemning the error of Origen, who argued that God's mercy would eventually free the demons from their punishment. Thomas says the Church has condemned this error for two reasons. First, according to Scripture, "the devil who had deceived them was thrown into the lake of fire and brimstone where the beast and the false prophet were, and they will be tormented day and night for ever and ever" (Rev. 20:10). Second, this error exaggerates God's mercy in one direction and depreciates it in another. It seems "equally reasonable" for good angels to remain in eternal happiness and bad angels in eternal unhappiness, yet Origen argued that as the bad angels would one day cease to suffer, so too would the good angels and the blessed someday cease to experience eternal happiness, instead returning to the state of unhappiness in this life.

As for objections, God's mercy is ruled "by the order of His wisdom." Some people, through their choices, *render themselves unworthy of His mercy*. This is the case for the damned and the demons. Still, *it can be said that God's mercy reaches even to them*, not in that their suffering ceases, but in that *they are punished less than they truly deserve* for having rejected God in His infinite goodness.

Are at least damned humans spared
from eternal punishment?

While the demons deserve eternal punishment, some believe that in His mercy, God will someday end the punishment of damned human beings. After all, in their charity, the saints pray for sinners in this life. In heaven, their charity will be even more perfect, so they will pray for the damned, and the prayers of the saints cannot be in vain. Further, the Psalms make it clear that God has not "in anger shut up his compassion" (77 [76]:9). God's anger is His punishment, so it follows that His punishment will not last forever.

Thomas points once again to Matthew 25:46: "They will go away into eternal punishment, but the righteous into eternal life." The reward of the just will never end, and neither will the punishment of the damned. St. John Damascene elaborated that "death is to men what their fall was to the angels." After their fall, the angels could not be restored; likewise, a man who dies in mortal sin cannot be spared from punishment. In commenting on this claim, Thomas cites Augustine, who showed how some avoided Origen's error by arguing that while the demons are punished forever, "all men, even unbelievers, are at length set free from punishment." This is an unreasonable view, because fallen angels are "obstinate in wickedness," as are "the souls of men who die without charity," as St. John Damascene demonstrated.

As for the prayers of the saints, Augustine and Gregory (saints themselves) both made clear that while on earth, the saints pray for the conversion even of their enemies. If they knew for certain that a sinner was "foreknown to death," they would no more pray for him than for the demons. Neither the Church Militant on earth nor the Church Triumphant in heaven prays for those whom God has justly damned. The apostle Paul made clear why we pray for the unrighteous *on earth*: "God may perhaps grant that they will repent and come to know the truth, and they may escape from the snare of the devil" (2 Tim. 2:25–26).

As for the passage from the Psalms on God's anger and compassion, this refers "to the vessels of mercy, which have not made themselves unworthy of mercy, because in this life (which may be called God's anger on account of its unhappiness), He changes vessels of mercy into something better." This is why the passage continues, "The right hand of the Most High has changed" (v. 10). Further, as noted before, God may display mercy not by ending the eternal punishment of the damned, but by diminishing its intensity compared with the suffering that the damned deserve for despising God's infinite goodness.

Does God's mercy bring an end to the punishment of Christians?

Perhaps, some suggest, while the punishment of demons and unbelievers will endure forever, the punishment of Christians may one day end. After all, Mark 16:16 says, "He who believes and is baptized will be saved; but he who does not believe will be condemned." Therefore, all Christians will eventually be saved because they believe in God and have been baptized. Christ Himself said, "He who eats my flesh and drinks my blood has eternal life" (John 6:54). Thomas explains, "Now this is the meat and drink whereof Christians partake in common. Therefore all Christians will be saved at length." (Readers will note that this objection was written more than two centuries before the Protestant Reformation.)

Thomas responds, to the contrary, with unambiguous words of the apostle Paul: "Do you not know that the unrighteous will not inherit the kingdom of God?" (1 Cor. 6:9). Some Christians are unrighteous; therefore, some will never inherit God's kingdom and will suffer eternally. Thomas also provides the sobering words of Christ's "rock," Peter: "It would have been better for them never to have known the way of righteousness than after knowing it to turn back from the holy commandment given to them" (2 Pet. 2:21). Those who do not know the way of truth will be punished forever, as will Christians who have turned back after knowing the way of righteousness.

Thomas elaborates with the wisdom of Augustine, who explained that some believed "whoever received the sacraments of faith would be immune from eternal punishment." This is not true, however, because some receive the sacrament of faith without having faith, and without faith, it is impossible to please God (Heb. 11:6). Others say those who receive the sacraments of faith and profess the Catholic Faith cannot not receive eternal punishment, but this runs contrary to the lesson from Peter that such persons deserve not a *lesser*, but a *greater* punishment.

As for the objections, only believers with a living "faith working through love" (Gal. 5:6) will be saved. This means that neither unbelievers nor Christians who have rejected God's loving charity and deadened their faith through mortal sin will escape eternal punishment. As for the saving power of the Eucharist, those who partake of it worthily, while united to God in charity, are brought to eternal life. One who receives it unworthily "eats and drinks judgment upon himself" (1 Cor. 11:29). Finally, "so far as the power of the sacrament is concerned, it brings us to eternal life, although sin may deprive us of that fruit, even after we have received worthily."

Will even the damned who performed acts
of mercy be punished eternally?

Here is a last, nuanced question regarding whether any among the damned will be pardoned. Scripture seems to indicate that those who perform acts of mercy cannot be eternally damned. James 2:13 says, "Judgment is without mercy to one who has shown no mercy; yet mercy triumphs over judgment." Further, consider Christ's teaching that "blessed are the merciful, for they shall obtain mercy" (Matt. 5:7); His instruction to pray, "Forgive us our debts, as we also have forgiven our debtors" (Matt. 6:12); and His promise that "if you forgive men their trespasses, your heavenly Father also will forgive you" (Matt. 6:14).

Thomas begins his response with the inspired words of St. Paul: "Neither the immoral, nor idolaters," and so forth, "will inherit the kingdom of God" (1 Cor. 6:9, 10). Now, many of the kinds of sinners Paul names do practice acts of mercy, so merciful acts, in themselves, do not free us from eternal punishment. We also read in Scripture that "whoever keeps the whole law but fails in one point has become guilty of all of it" (James 2:10). Therefore, whoever keeps the law regarding works of mercy, but fails to keep it by committing mortally sinful acts, is guilty of transgressing the law and will be punished eternally.

We must recall that "in the absence of charity," nothing is acceptable to God or of "profit unto eternal life." Some people who are not united to God in the love of charity still perform merciful acts for various other reasons. A clear example would be a person who acquires great wealth unjustly and then distributes some of his ill-gotten gains to the poor. Such merciful acts do not merit heaven, because they are bereft of charity. Thomas says we must conclude that "neither faith nor works of mercy will free from eternal punishment" all who die in mortal sin, "not even after any length of time whatever."

As for the arguments to the contrary, Thomas explains that the passages from James and Matthew regarding the merciful mean that "those will obtain mercy who show mercy in an ordinate manner." In other words, mercy does not avail a person who has been merciful to another inordinately, that is, while neglecting the welfare of his own soul through unrepented mortal sin. Such acts of mercy may *lessen* his punishment, but cannot *free* him from it. As for Christ's words in the Gospel of Matthew, Thomas concludes: "Our Lord said this to those who ask that their debt be forgiven, but not to those who persist in sin. Wherefore the repentant alone will obtain by their works of mercy the forgiveness that sets them free altogether."

38

Last Thoughts on the Last Things: Hell

*God predestines no one to hell; for this, a willful
turning away from God (a mortal sin) is necessary,
and persistence in it until the end.*

—CCC 1037

Our *Catechism* briefly, but profoundly discusses hell in paragraphs
1033–1037. The Church confirms Thomas's teaching on the existence of hell and its eternal fire, adding, "The chief punishment
of hell is eternal separation from God, in whom alone man can
possess the life and happiness for which he was created and for
which he longs" (1035). Here, we see what Thomas described
as the damned's experience of the unbearable grief that comes
from having lost the greatest of all possible goods through one's
own willful obstinance.

It can certainly be a frightful thing to read of the utter and
unending despair of the damned. Indeed, Thomas tells us that
every faculty and every bit of knowledge they possess will only
add to their unhappiness. Such thoughts should indeed inspire
healthy fear of the Lord and dread of "the loss of heaven and
the pains of hell," which we express in the Act of Contrition
after Confession.

Nonetheless, as we see in our opening quotation, the *Catechism* makes clear that "God predestines no one to hell." Sadly for the damned, the gates of hell are indeed open only to those who choose to walk through them by persisting in mortal sin, despite the graces God offers us to one day join Him forever in heaven.

Thomas writes again and again of the relentless "obstinacy" of the damned that perpetually "enchains" them. I'll offer just a few thoughts that the idea of eternal obstinacy in the wicked provokes in me. I'll borrow first from a pagan philosopher, a well-known modern Christian apologist, and finally from our own Angelic Doctor.

The Stoic philosopher Epictetus posed this rhetorical question: "When a man who has been trapped in an argument hardens to stone, how shall one any longer deal with him by argument?"[114] Here on earth, and even regarding earthly matters, people who are particularly stubborn or obstinate are unwilling to admit they are wrong. Sometimes, they even refuse to be open to rational discussion with others of different views who might guide them to important truths that could greatly improve their lot.[115] Their pride traps them.

In a sense, those who are obstinate in mortal sin have chosen to hear the voice of the devil and have hardened their hearts to the good news of Christ. Perhaps we see a glimpse of this even in

---

[114] Epictetus, *Discourses*, bks. 3–4, *Fragments*, *The Encheiridion*, trans. W. A. Oldfather, Loeb Classical Library 218 (Cambridge, MA: Harvard University Press, 2000), 483.

[115] Sadly, as I write in September 2020, so much of what used to be free political debate and discussion seems to be increasingly petrified due to intellectual obstinacy and refusal to consider and acknowledge differing viewpoints.

the pagan mythology of the ancient Greeks, who held that those who stared into the face of the most evil, beastly Gorgon were literally turned to stone. We might consider a biblical parallel in Lot's wife, who contradicted a direct order from God, and looking back upon Sodom and Gomorrah, "she became a pillar of salt" (Gen. 19:26). The obstinate harden their hearts, and only living, moving, loving hearts can ever be one with God.

As for the modern Christian apologist, I wonder who among my readers has read C. S. Lewis's delightful little novel *The Great Divorce*. The divorce of which Lewis writes is not between a human couple, but between heaven and hell, which are separated by a great divide. In Lewis's tale, a busload of people from hell take a day trip to heaven. Lewis portrays so well how completely and resolutely those folks down below have chosen their own eternal destination by obstinately and irrevocably rejecting God's mercy.

As for insights on how some people choose hell, we turn now to our own Angelic Doctor. In the Second Part of the Second Part of the *Summa*, question 14, Thomas considers the sins against the Holy Spirit as he explicates Church teaching on these most striking words of Christ: "Whoever speaks against the Holy Spirit will not be forgiven, either in this age or in the age to come" (Matt. 12:32; see Mark 3:29 and Luke 12:10).

Now, I recall learning during the years of atheism in my youth that some prominent twentieth-century critics of Christianity, including the renowned British philosopher Bertrand Russell, wrote that these words from the Gospels have caused untold misery to Christians throughout the ages by making them wonder whether, at some point, they might have inadvertently committed such a sin and forfeited their salvation in exchange for eternal damnation. If only Russell (and my younger self) had known that first, it just doesn't work that way, and second, St. Thomas Aquinas had explained those words in great detail centuries earlier.

Blasphemy of the Holy Spirit does not happen accidentally; in fact, it takes considerable malevolent intention. God's mercy is so great that we must actively work against it if we wish to forfeit it completely and render ourselves, as Thomas stated in his "Treatise on the Resurrection," "unworthy of His mercy." Thomas explains Church teaching on *six* sins against the Holy Spirit (*ST*, II-II, 14, 3). Here they are in brief:

1. *Despair.* This is the complete abandonment of hope in one's salvation through God's goodness, which amounts to the denial or rejection of the power of God's mercy.

2. *Presumption.* Paragraph 2092 of the *Catechism* tells us that we may commit the sin of presumption either by being overconfident in our own ability to earn salvation without God's help, or by believing that God will grant us our salvation without any effort on our part.

3. *Impugning the known truth.* This means willfully and actively to attack, contradict, distort, or falsify spiritual matter we know to be true.

4. *Envy of another's spiritual good.* The opposite of loving charity, envy begrudges another his hope of happiness and salvation. We might recall Thomas's words that "envy reigns supreme in the damned."

5. *Obstinacy in sin.* This means stubbornly refusing the power and gifts of the Holy Spirit. It might include willful ignorance of virtue and refusal to fight against our vices.

6. *Final impenitence.* A most profoundly grave and sad sin, final impenitence is man's persistent and explicit

rejection of God and His mercy. It is an unwillingness to be contrite, to seek out forgiveness, and to have regret, shame, or remorse for our sins.

Clearly, such sins are not inadvertent oversights arising through unintended negligence or the temporary insanity of some overriding passion of the moment. They cannot come into or remain in our hearts without our own explicit and willful permission.

Let's conclude with our last thoughts on hell, for now, with a profoundly important lesson from the *Catechism*: "There are no limits to the mercy of God, but anyone who deliberately refuses to accept his mercy by repenting, rejects the forgiveness of his sins and the salvation offered by the Holy Spirit" (1864).

Conclusion

Faith, Hope, Love, and the Four Things That Last

In my Father's house are many rooms; if it were not so,
would I have told you that I go to prepare a place for you?

—John 14:2

Love never ends.

—1 Corinthians 13:8

Faith: The Foundation of Our Mansions in Heaven

Jesus Christ Himself told us that He has prepared a room (a mansion, in the translation Thomas used) for each one of us (John 14:2), if we but believe in Him and be baptized (Mark 16:16); eat His flesh and drink His blood (John 6:54); take up His yoke, follow Him, and rest in Him (Matt. 11:28–30); and show our love for Him by keeping His commandments (John 14:15), the greatest of which is to love God with all we are, and our neighbors as ourselves (Matt. 22:37–39; Mark 12:29–31; Luke 10:27).

Faith provides the foundation of the dwelling Christ has prepared for us in heaven, should we choose to accept His invitation and persevere to the end (Matt. 24:13). Faith is the first of three theological virtues of faith, hope, and love (or charity) that Paul enumerates (1 Cor. 13:13). Thomas expounds on all three over the course of more than two hundred pages in the Second Part of the Second Part of his great *Summa Theologica*. These theological virtues transcend and perfect the *natural* virtues (temperance, fortitude, justice, and prudence) that perfect our human nature. The theological virtues are *supernatural* virtues, bestowed through God's grace in our souls through the sacrament of Baptism, and enhanced by the other sacraments of Christ's Church.

Faith, the first theological virtue, is far more than merely a rational belief *that God exists*, (which belief, Thomas has shown so well, is indeed mandated by reason). It entails a personal relationship with God and an acceptance of His freely offered grace. It transcends natural virtue and natural acts of religion, or worship of God. Per Thomas, "God is the object of faith, not only because we believe in a God, but because we believe God."[116] Further, the virtue of faith "is a habit of the mind, whereby eternal life is begun in us, making the intellect assent to what is non-apparent."[117] By embracing God's gift of faith, our eternal life begins *now*.

Let's note that there is an intellectual component to faith, in that faith assents to the invisible, supernatural truths of God. This implies that we should seek to grow in our Faith, to learn the essential articles of faith, and to deepen our level of understanding throughout our lives. Thankfully, God has given us not only the inspired words of Scripture, but also the Catholic Church herself, with all her saints, Fathers, and Doctors, to help us fathom the richness and interconnectedness of the great truths of faith.

[116] *ST*, II-II, 81, 5.
[117] *ST*, II-II, 4, 1.

Each of us will build the foundation of his heavenly mansion by becoming humble, as Christ taught, and by following Thomas's example of learning and cherishing the great labors the Fathers and Doctors of the Church have undertaken over the centuries to ferret out the deep, mysterious, and multiple senses of Scripture and to build a sure grasp of the articles of faith.

Hope: Be Not Afraid!

Surely, Thomas's explanations of the eternal agonies of hell, and even of the temporary sufferings incurred through the cleansing fires of purgatory, will give all of us pause. Perhaps some will have a dreadful fear of great pains to come. Still, warranted fears should not prove paralyzing or lead anyone into despair or scrupulosity. Though the stakes of the game of life on earth could not be higher, God gives us everything we need to win the prize (1 Cor. 9:24), if only we are willing to accept His assistance and die in a state of grace. Consider the words repeated hundreds of times throughout Scripture, words that would become a motto of Pope St. John Paul II: "Be not afraid!" One of the greatest graces God gives us on earth to remove our fears and fortify our souls is the second theological virtue: hope.

Hope is integrally connected to our desired last end of eternal life in heaven. Thomas says, "In so far as we hope for anything as being possible to us by means of the Divine assistance, our hope attains God Himself, on Whose help it leans."[118] Through hope, we look forward to spending eternity with God — and trust that He will provide us with what we need to get there! When thinking of the Last Things, we should never fear excessively or

---

[118] *ST*, II-II, 17, 1.

fail to remember that we have reason to rejoice if we cling to our hope in God's justice and mercy, for "the proper and principal object of hope is eternal happiness."[119]

Further, we should recall Thomas's words cited in the prologue to part 1 of this book: "For if man had no hope of another, better life after death, without doubt death would be very dreadful, and man would commit any wicked deed rather than taste death. But since we believe that there is another, better life to which we shall come after death, it is evident that no one should fear death or do anything wrong through fear of death." Be not afraid!

Love: Accepting God's Offer of Eternal Friendship

"So faith, hope, love abide, these three; but the greatest of these is love" (1 Cor. 13:13). Faith and hope are wonderful and indispensable gifts as we live life on earth, but they are both brought to life and surpassed in their splendor by the theological virtue of charity (*caritas* in Thomas's Latin), or love. Indeed, says Thomas, "the principal act of charity ... is to love,"[120] and he begins his great "Treatise on Charity" by showing how charity is really a state of friendship between man and God. John 15:15 says, "No longer do I call you servants ... but I have called you friends," and 1 Corinthians 1:9 adds, "God is faithful, by whom you were called into the fellowship of his Son, Jesus Christ our Lord."

Thomas elaborates by citing Augustine: "By charity I mean the movement of the soul towards the enjoyment of God for His own sake."[121] God supernaturally implants this love within

---

[119] *ST*, II-II, 17, 2.
[120] *ST*, II-II, 27, prologue.
[121] Cited in *ST*, II-II, 23, 2.

our hearts, so that through the movement of our will by the Holy Spirit, "the love of charity is the root of merit." If we die infused with God's charity, not having separated ourselves from it through unrepented mortal sin, we are graced to merit eternal life in heaven.

Indeed, echoing St. Paul's words on the greatness of charity, Thomas proclaims charity the "mother" of all virtues, since "every virtue depends on it in a way."[122] Even the theological virtues of faith and hope require charity for their perfection. Recall these words from Scripture: "You believe that God is one; you do well. Even the demons believe — and shudder" (James 2:19). St. James also tells us, "For as the body apart from the spirit is dead, so faith apart from works is dead" (2:26). Thomas writes of both "lifeless faith" and "living faith." What is it that produces the works that "quicken" faith and make it come alive? According to Thomas, "Each thing works through its form. Now faith works through charity. Therefore the love of charity is the form of faith."[123]

The love of charity perfects hope as well. The virtue of hope opens our souls to the Holy Spirit's gift of fear of the Lord, which helps us desire the good and avoid the evils that would deprive us of it. Fear of the Lord at its lowest level is called *servile* fear, whereby we fear God's punishment for our sins. The reasonable fear of the pains of hell and purgatory is a good place to begin. Indeed, Scripture tells us again and again that fear of the Lord is fundamental to wisdom (Job 28:28; Ps. 111 [110]:10; Prov. 15:33; Sir. 1:14). Yet as we grow in virtue and spiritual union with God, our *servile* fear is transformed into a higher, *filial* fear,

---

[122] *ST*, II-II, 23, 4. (You may recall that even acts of mercy are not meritorious unless prompted by charity, as we saw earlier.)
[123] *ST*, II-II, 4, 3.

a fear of committing a fault not merely because we will suffer, but because it offends God. And what perfects this fear of the Lord? The First Letter of John (4:18) says, "Fear has to do with punishment, and he who fears is not perfected in love." Indeed, per the same verse, "perfect love casts out fear." If we embrace God in the perfect love He has invited us to share with Him, we need not fear our eternal fate, for we will share it with Him who graced us with such love.

Four Things That Last Forever

We have considered aplenty Thomas's carefully worded wisdom on the Four Last Things of death, judgment, heaven, and hell, and we just took a brief look at some of Thomas's insights on faith, hope, and charity. I will conclude by offering a few last thoughts on *four things that will last forever.*

1. *Love.* "God is love" (1 John 4:8), and God is eternal (Deut. 33:27; Isa. 40:28; 1 Tim. 1:17). Further, among the theological virtues, Thomas explains that only charity will last forever. We will not need faith in "things unseen" (Heb. 11:1) once we see them clearly, "face to face," and not "in a mirror dimly" as we do now (1 Cor. 13:12). Neither will those in heaven need to hope to reach their ultimate end, since they will already have arrived! (And sadly, those who choose hell will have no hope of leaving it.)

2. *Heaven.* Death, in the sense of the separation of our immortal souls from our corruptible bodies, will not last forever. At the time of the Last Judgment, as Thomas has thoroughly explained, our souls will be reunited with our bodies. And indeed, we have seen

that the Last Judgment itself may be over in an instant, but the execution of God's judgment will endure forever. For those who die united to God in loving charity, the final result will be eternal life in heaven in the company of the saints and angels, who rejoice in the love of God. Blessed with glorified bodies, the saints will enjoy forever the Beatific Vision of God in His essence, the source and font of all truth, love, beauty, and goodness.

3. *Hate.* Hate will endure forever, but only for those who ultimately choose to hate God and to reject His love by living and dying in the charity-destroying thrall of mortal sin. Thomas has explained how, while on earth, we can be well served by a proper passion of hatred, by which we hate things that keep us from what we love. If we love God, our neighbor, and the God-given good within our own bodies and souls, we will hate sin and work to avoid or destroy it. Yet if we die in mortal sin, having rejected the loving charity of God, we will have only hate, without any love or any possible good to achieve by it. Thomas tells us that "envy reigns supreme in the damned," and envy is hatred of another person's good.

4. *Hell.* Hell is that last and everlasting thing that remains for all who reject God's pure and generous love, choosing instead Satan's tainted, petty, and self-destroying hate. They will have only that false mockery of love, the kind of "love" that "loves" the miserable company of other damned souls and the demons.

I'll conclude with my hope and prayer that the insights of the Scriptures, the *Catechism*, and the teaching of the great Fathers and Doctors of the Church—St. Thomas Aquinas the foremost among them—have helped inspire in you further awe of the power, wisdom, goodness, love, justice, and mercy of God. May you strive to love Him more dearly with all that you are, and may you and your loved ones, with a hope inflamed with charity, look forward to eternal life in the unspeakable bliss of that last and everlasting thing of the Beatific Vision of God in heaven.

About the Author

Kevin Vost obtained his Doctor of Psychology in Clinical Psychology from Adler University in Chicago with internship and dissertation research at the Southern Illinois University School of Medicine, Alzheimer's Center, Memory and Aging Clinic.

Dr. Vost has taught psychology and gerontology at Aquinas College in Nashville, the University of Illinois at Springfield, MacMurray College, and Lincoln Land Community College. He has served as a Research Review Committee Member for American Mensa and as an Advisory Board Member for the International Association of Resistance Trainers.

He is the author of twenty Catholic books, and his hobbies include lifting big weights and reading big books, such as those of St. Thomas Aquinas. He resides with his wife and their two dogs in Springfield, Illinois.

Sophia Institute

Sophia Institute is a nonprofit institution that seeks to nurture the spiritual, moral, and cultural life of souls and to spread the Gospel of Christ in conformity with the authentic teachings of the Roman Catholic Church.

Sophia Institute Press fulfills this mission by offering translations, reprints, and new publications that afford readers a rich source of the enduring wisdom of mankind.

Sophia Institute also operates the popular online resource CatholicExchange.com. *Catholic Exchange* provides world news from a Catholic perspective as well as daily devotionals and articles that will help readers to grow in holiness and live a life consistent with the teachings of the Church.

In 2013, Sophia Institute launched Sophia Institute for Teachers to renew and rebuild Catholic culture through service to Catholic education. With the goal of nurturing the spiritual, moral, and cultural life of souls, and an abiding respect for the role and work of teachers, we strive to provide materials and programs that are at once enlightening to the mind and ennobling to the heart; faithful and complete, as well as useful and practical.

Sophia Institute gratefully recognizes the Solidarity Association for preserving and encouraging the growth of our apostolate over the course of many years. Without their generous and timely support, this book would not be in your hands.

www.SophiaInstitute.com
www.CatholicExchange.com
www.SophiaInstituteforTeachers.org

Sophia Institute Press® is a registered trademark of Sophia Institute.
Sophia Institute is a tax-exempt institution as defined by the
Internal Revenue Code, Section 501(c)(3). Tax ID 22-2548708.